LOW-COST
EMERGENCY PLANNING

A DIY GUIDE TO FAMILY DISASTER PREPAREDNESS

JULIE L. JESSEPH-BALAA
FOREWORD BY ED BEGLEY JR.

Skyhorse Publishing

Skyhorse Publishing books may be purchased in bulk at special discounts
for sales promotion, corporate gifts, fund-raising, or educational
purposes. Special editions can also be created to specifications. For
details, contact the Special Sales Department, Skyhorse Publishing,
307 West 36th Street, 11th Floor, New York, NY 10018 or info@
skyhorsepublishing.com.

Skyhorse® and Skyhorse Publishing® are registered trademarks of
Skyhorse Publishing, Inc.®, a Delaware corporation.

www.skyhorsepublishing.com.

Cover design by Kai Texel
Front cover images by Getty Images and Julie L. Jesseph-Balaa
Back cover image by Racina Balaa

10 9 8 7 6 5 4 3 2 1

Library of Congress Cataloging-in-Publication Data is available on file.

ISBN: 978-1-5107-5860-5
Ebook ISBN: 978-1-5107-7506-0

Printed in China

CONTENTS

Foreword

Julie Jesseph-Balaa has created a remarkable low-cost guide to living better on less. She demonstrates that you don't have to be wealthy to be self-sufficient—you can tone things down and do more with less, as Julie shows here. This path to self-reliance and advice for how we can all be prepared for future emergencies is deeply inspiring.

She built her own greenhouse, grows food and sells it to the community at the farmers market, raises bees in the city, collects rain, and teaches her students how to recycle everything and to get involved in the community. These things don't cost money, they just take time and commitment. Her lively book also tells us about cooking with the sun, making and repairing our own clothes, and how to be more prepared simply by using manual tools. And there's so much more here!

This wonderful book reads both like a diary and a how-to guide for anyone wanting to follow in her footsteps. This book makes me feel even more prepared.

—Ed Begley Jr., Actor and Environmental Activist

Acknowledgments

I am grateful for the efforts and work done by many people through the educational, non-profit, community-service corporation White Tower Inc. (WTI), with their pioneering thinking and experimentation and application of solutions for humankind. Richard E. White nobly began that corporation partly to share how we can all take the "highest and best" approach to our lives. His knowledge of "Universal Principles" uplifted my life and mentality and also showed many people how to think, study, and research scientifically and how to act ethically, morally, spiritually, and lovingly. As Richard E. White said, "There is no greater gift than an upright example!"

It is to Richard E. White—and to all those who seek better ways to address and live within our human condition—that I dedicate this book.

I humbly thank brotherly friend Christopher Nyerges for ceaselessly supporting me in following through with completing this guide. My appreciation to editor Sarah Janssen for gracious assistance with this book.

I'm grateful for my husband and friend, Talal Balaa, for his wonderful moral support, and for writing the solar article and working together on organizing the photos; for Racina Balaa, who also supportively jumped in to assist on this journey and generously contributed her artful photography in this collaborative production. Thank you, forward-thinker Gabriel Balaa, for your positive comments, availability, and for being a source of inspiration in my thinking.

Thank you, Ed Begley Jr., for your support and participation!

Thanks to Prudence Boczarski and Patience Kay for providing photos of their endeavors with self-employment and of their skills and talents. Thanks also to Pascal Baudar, for your contributions teaching pickling; Ellen Hall, for sharing food storage system data; Art Lee, for contributing first aid kit instructions; and to many others not mentioned here, who contributed to this book.

Introduction

It is always best to be prepared for anything that may confront us. The purpose of this book is to be a guide to our getting ready, and living ready, now.

Imagine that your world has crumbled! Everything you took for granted is not functioning, or it's gone, at least temporarily. You still need to survive and to function daily.

War, famine, economic collapse, tidal waves, natural disasters, a comet hitting the earth, terrorist attacks—any of these possibilities could degrade the day-to-day functions that you depend upon to get food, water, money, and supplies. If suddenly thousands of people were killed, their jobs won't get done, and that might affect your life and your town. The scenarios are many, and the more prepared you are, the better.

This book will teach you how to be prepared for emergencies, especially if you're on a budget. But it's not only about being prepared for emergencies. This text is all about how to live—ecologically and economically. You'll find that if that is your focus, you will be better prepared for emergencies, and your life will be more meaningful, and more fulfilling.

Each of us can do a lot to reach this goal by adjusting how we live our own lives and interact with one another. We need to remember becoming prepared is an ongoing activity. It can be a great joy and accomplishment, which you can share with your family, neighbors, and friends. Preparation is a mental outlook and a way of systemized and principled living. Learn, apply, and share these basic strategies, and you will have an action plan and a good foundation.

I have, at times, felt that taking action seemed difficult and uncomfortable, or even painful, yet once you get started it is actually a joy. Let's embrace our need to be prepared, one step at a time, methodically, starting with the basics!

Chapter 1
Water

View of the California Aqueduct.
(Photo by Getty Images.)

E ven in the direst situation, you need water. It is the most essential element for life. Let's assume that there's no water flowing when you turn on your faucet. Now what?

Let's explore where you might find your water. We'll begin in the post-emergency city, and we'll also consider some wilderness options.

IN A NUTSHELL

- Finding local water
- Collecting water
- Water purification methods
- Home water storage
- Recycling household water

FINDING LOCAL WATER

Do you know where your water comes from? Most people don't.

If you live in a rural area, you may have a well for your water source, or perhaps a local lake or spring. It's good to know where your water comes from, since water is the one resource that we cannot do without.

When my husband and I sat down and looked at a map of our neighborhood in Los Angeles, we started to note the various water features listed on the map, things like rivers (yes, there are rivers that flow through the L.A. area), lakes, reservoirs, springs, and even some streams in the nearby mountains. But where does everyone get their drinking water, the water that flows into the sink of every house in the vast multi-million population metropolis where we live?

With a bit of research, we discovered that about 26 percent of the water for Los Angeles is obtained locally. Only 26 percent! That means that about 74 percent of the water comes from somewhere else. As we

Samantha Bode, filmmaker, along the California Aqueduct. Bode walked the entire three-hundred-plus miles of the aqueduct over two months and created *The Longest Straw* documentary.

continued our research, we learned there are three major aqueducts that feed water into Los Angeles County, bringing in water from over three hundred miles away. Two of the aqueducts bring water from Mono Lake to the north. The third aqueduct brings in water from the Colorado River to the east.

A topographical map of your area tells you where to find local water. All water features are in blue.

As we began to ponder the deeper significance of these facts, we realized that for all the sprawling population of Los Angeles with its voracious water appetite, only one-quarter of that water is found nearby, in the local foothills of the local mountains. We felt concerned about what might happen as the population continues to grow, or what might happen if an earthquake cut off that water supply.

Of course, there are many things that are out of our control in our environments. But everyone, wherever they live, should learn where their water comes from. A topographical map is an ideal map to use to see where water is located in your neighborhood. US Geological Survey (USGS) topographical maps show the contours of the landscape and all the water features, including springs, reservoirs, permanent rivers, and seasonal rivers.

If you don't want to buy a paper full-color map from the USGS, you could also go onto Google Maps and study your local area, using the "terrain" feature.

I strongly suggest that you study whatever map you choose and make a note of the location of all reservoirs, swimming pools, rivers, springs, and water features where you actually might be able to get water in an emergency.

It would be wise to learn all the features near and far from your home, for the sake of knowing. But also consider that if you really had to haul some water home, perhaps while walking, you might be able to carry a five-gallon bucket in each hand but you probably wouldn't fill each one entirely. You want a bucket in each hand for balance. You'll see what I mean if you try carrying a heavy weight in only one hand for any distance. It's very hard, and an equal weight in each hand would be much easier.

Person carrying heavy water buckets. (Photo by Racina Balaa.)

Let's say you filled each bucket with three gallons of water. That's six gallons total, and since each gallon weighs 8.3 pounds, each bucket will weigh 24.9 pounds. You'd be carrying nearly 50 pounds if you have just three gallons in each hand. Could you do that? How far would you be able to walk with that much weight?

On your map of your area, study it for all the places where water might be captured or held. Reservoirs are everywhere, and these are potential sources of water, obviously. But everyone else in town might know about the reservoirs, so consider the risks of exposure and go to the reservoir with friends.

RIVERS

Rivers and streams flow through many towns and even big cities, but as the water gets into the heart of the city, it's usually underground or flowing through a hidden pipe. Again, if you study a topographical map of your area, you can learn where the waterways run. An older map of your city might even show you where the rivers once existed above ground, and this is often a clue to finding water. One source of old maps might be a local historical society.

A river that flows through an urban area. The freeway is above.

WILDERNESS OPTIONS

In rural and wilderness areas, you can find springs, streams (seasonal and permanent), rivers, lakes, ice, snow, and of course, rain.

Springs tend to be the purest source of water, since they typically flow out of rock, and the water is not open and exposed, and therefore not subject to pollution.

When there are no obvious natural sources of water, you still have a few options.

SWIMMING POOLS

In cities and suburbs, there are likely swimming pools. These will hold water for some time after a disaster, and the water can be used. Remember, the closer to your home or base of operations the better, because water weighs about 8 pounds a gallon, and that can really add up. It would be a good idea to get to know all your close neighbors who have swimming pools. In an emergency where there is no water flowing in the city pipes, you could use that pool water, once treated.

Of course, all that water is probably chlorinated, and health authorities always suggest that you not consume such water. That's good advice, but we're talking about a situation where you might not have any other water. Keep in mind that the sunlight degrades the chlorine in the water, and then straining and boiling the water will make it a bit more palatable.

Swimming pools are emergency sources of water.

Yes, pool water may be useful for some things, but converting it to safe, pure water will take effort.

So here are some general guidelines:

- Pool water can be used as-is to wash the feet and body—murky is better than nothing.
- Do you have sunshine? Letting the pool water sit in sunlight will cause chlorine to dissipate, and the sun's UV rays will kill undesirable organisms. At the end of the sunshine treatment, that water will be cleaner than when you started.
- Filter water through layers of clean cloth, and then boil the water for a full minute (after it reaches a rolling boil) for drinking and cooking. Boiling will kill bacteria and viruses; chemicals and metals will not be removed.

Ornamental fountains are similar to pools and can be another good emergency source of water, at least initially. These can be found in residential areas, public gardens, and even commercial areas. The more you know about your area the better.

HOUSEHOLD SOURCES

Nearly every home has a water heater, and this might contain 30 to 40 gallons of usable water. Other home sources of water include toilet tanks, ice cubes, and obviously any stored water at the home.

You should go through your entire household and look for all the sources of water that you already have—water heater, ice cubes, toilet tank, swimming pool, fountains, waterbed, etc. But remember, those emergency sources are the source of water you will use only if you didn't think beyond the moment. It's good to know about those emergency sources of water. But you should also know about more regular sources of water, and how to store water. (We'll get to water storage in a few pages.)

RAIN

"Wilderness" and "Urban" are not always clean distinctions. Both environments receive rain? If it's raining and you need water, be sure to put out your rain buckets. In the urban setting, your roof is your "collector," and all the rain that hits the roof drains to the gutters, and down to the downspouts. It's easy to get 30 gallons of rain in a downpour.

The first water from a storm will usually be dirty, full of all manner of debris washing off your roof, leaves, and even bird feces. So let the first half-hour of rain clean your roof and then start collecting for consumption. In any case, wait for 30 minutes of a rain so that the pollutants in the air have been removed by the rainfall.

How do you process rainwater? Let it settle, and then carefully scoop it out of your bucket, cup by cup, and filter it through a fine cotton cloth.

This is a simple method. Put a funnel on top of the storage bottles (usually one-gallon glass or plastic) and place a tightly woven, high thread-count cotton cloth into the funnel. The tightly woven cloth helps to collect any fine debris in the water. Then boil the water before use, in the slight chance that biological contaminants have gotten into the water.

Local historian Kevin Sutherland with a rain collection barrel positioned to collect rain that drains off the roof.

One method to capture rainwater, so any debris is automatically filtered.

If your rainwater looks like dark tea, it might still be OK to drink if you really have nothing else, but you might consider using it for something else.

If you're planning to use the roof of your home or garage to collect rain, you should make a point to keep the roof and gutters clean. One of the easiest ways to do this is to coat the roof with a white liquid rubber. We used Henry's Solarflex 287, though this is just one of many options. This product was originally developed to keep mobile home roofs cooler. Still, this product will seal leaks in any roof, and it will clean quickly in the first rain. A roof coated with this product will last longer and produce cleaner rain for your use.

Prudence filters rainwater.

Henry's® roofing product keeps the roof cleaner, so the collected runoff is cleaner.

You can collect rainwater in any containers, but clean recycled buckets, cans, and bottles are all free! We've used large trash cans, and pickle barrels. Place a window screen across the top of the barrel to prevent leaves and debris from dropping into the container.

Once the rainwater is collected, don't just let it sit there and breed mosquitoes. Cover the container when it is full. Then, once any fine particulate matter in the rain has settled in your container, siphon or dip it out. Run it through a water filter if you feel the need. Then store it in clean containers.

One-gallon glass jugs are a good water storage container. You can reuse them for free, and glass is inert, so there is no leaching of particulate plastic into the water. Plus, glass lasts "forever" (assuming you don't break it). Secure them by packing the glass jugs into wooden boxes or milk crates, with a little bubble wrap around each jug.

Julie putting water containers into a safe box.

Julie cuts plastic bubble wrap to wrap glass jars for storage. This will help prevent breakage.

A WELL

Yes, you can simply dig a well, but just like with real estate, everything concerning a well is about location, location, and location. If you must dig a well, dig it in a dry stream bed (water was once running there), and dig it on the inside of a curve, where the water would likely slow, and settle.

Though it's not impossible to find water this way in urban areas, it's unlikely in most cities. But it's really a matter of your location. I recommend that you obtain a topographical map for your location, and study it for your local water features. Go to usgs.gov. Or talk to a local geologist.

SOLAR STILL

The desert solar still is another way to extract water from the soil. It's not something you do on a regular basis—this is an emergency measure.

Here are some general guidelines:

1. Dig a hole in a suitable place.
2. Put a container in the middle of the hole.
3. Cover the hole with a sheet of plastic.
4. Put a pebble in the middle so the plastic forms an inverted cone.
5. As water evaporates out of the soil, it is trapped on the bottom side of the plastic and drips back into your container to be collected.

Students make a desert solar still in the attempt to extract water from the soil.

TRANSPIRATION BAG

This is a simple, but desperation-level, means of water collection. Place a clear plastic bag—the bigger the better—over tree branches that are exposed to the sun. It must be a tree that does not have toxic leaves. (Willow trees are ideal for this.) After a few hours, or a day, water will be trapped in the bag.

This transpiration bag, on a willow tree for about twenty-four hours, produced over a quart of water.

WATER PURIFICATION METHODS

FIRE AND HEAT

Fire is the best way to kill biological contaminants that might be in water. You just need a pot and the ability to get a fire going. One way to do this is to just make a circle of bricks, and lay a grill over it. This creates a primitive stove for boiling water or cooking.

However, you should get a simple barbecue stove, or other backyard stove that you can power with wood, so you always have a way to boil water and cook food in the back yard. These stoves are inexpensively obtained at thrift stores or yard sales.

How long must you boil to kill all organisms? Since everything that gets you sick is dead at 160 to 170 degrees Fahrenheit, water is good to go once you bring it to a boil. (There are some rare exceptions to this.)

THE SUN

You can also purify your water from the sun. The water is purified by a combination of the sun's UV rays and its heat.

The simplest method for cleaning rainwater or other water: pour the water through a heavy cotton cloth.

You can fill up quart-sized glass jars and place them in the sun for a low-tech pasteurization. In general, about six hours in full sun is adequate for pasteurization. In this case, the UV rays sterilize the water.

SODIS

Are there any plastic liter bottles around? This is another of those ubiquitous bits of trash that you find just about everywhere in today's world. A plastic bottle can also be used for water purification, in a method called SODIS that is widely practiced in countries where there is no safe water infrastructure.

According to various international agencies, such as EAWAG (Swiss Federal Institute of Environmental Science and Technology) and SANDEC (Department of Water Sanitation in Developing Countries), clear plastic water bottles can serve a valuable role in disinfecting water.

SODIS is short for solar disinfection, a method of purifying water in clear plastic containers by placing them in the sunlight.

SODIS is an initialism for SOlar water DISinfection. SODIS takes advantage of the sun's UV rays and the process of pasteurization. Here is one simple SODIS method:

1. Select a clear PET plastic bottle, free of scratches and dirt. (PET is short for polyethylene terephthalate, the chemical name for polyester.)

2. Fill the bottle three-quarters full of clear water and shake to aerate. (If the collected water is cloudy or contains suspended debris, it should first be allowed to settle in another container, like a bucket. Then the water should be strained through a cloth before being poured into the plastic bottle.)

3. Fill the bottle the rest of the way and secure the lid tightly.

4. Expose the water to the sun by laying the bottles on their side

somewhere where shadows will not be cast on them, ideally on a corrugated metal roof.

5. Allow about six hours of exposure during full sunlight before you drink the water.

Adequate sunlight is necessary for this to work, and obviously, takes longer in the winter when the sun is lower. Cloud cover also means you'll have to keep the bottles in the sun longer than the recommended six hours.

HOW LONG IN THE SUN?

- Six hours if the sky is cloudless or up to 50 percent cloudy.
- Two consecutive days if the sky is more than 50 percent cloudy.
- One hour at a water temperature of at least 122 degrees Fahrenheit.

During days of continuous rainfall, SODIS does not perform satisfactorily. Rainwater harvesting or boiling is recommended during these days.

Standing bottles upright does not work as well as laying them on their sides. And for maximum effectiveness, you don't want water deeper than ten centimeters (just under four inches) for ideal UV penetration.

SODIS is an excellent choice if you cannot draw attention to yourself with a fire, or in the aftermath of an emergency where you have some plastic bottles but not much else. You also won't need to expend the energy of searching for firewood.

For more research on SODIS, go to: http://www.sodis.ch/methode/ anwendung/ausbildungsmaterial/dokumente_material/manual_e.pdf

MAKESHIFT WATER FILTERS

If you have a conventional water filter, use it!

But if not, you can use a coffee, beer, or soda can for a makeshift water filter.

Cut off the top of the can, and punch little holes into the bottom of the can. You then pack the inside of the can with something that will collect debris and contaminants in the water.

Various filtering agents that have been experimented with are clean sand mixed with a bit of charcoal (charcoal is the primary purification agent), or clean cotton, such as clean socks (or other fabric that can be packed tightly into the can).

A filter like this cannot be expected to be 100 percent effective, but it can help to remove some contaminants from the water.

Begin a makeshift filter by punching holes in the bottom of a can.

HOME WATER STORAGE

WATER CONTAINERS, AND HOW TO GET THEM FOR FREE

For most people, storing water is a part of their emergency planning, unless you happen to live next to a lake or river. In an emergency, you want to have water near your home—and kitchen and bathroom—when you need it. You don't want to haul a bucket from a water source each time you want water, do you?

So, what containers do you use for water storage? You can go to

Pour water through the makeshift filter, capturing the filtered water in a clean container below.

any home improvement store and buy buckets. They are under $10 each for a five-gallon bucket with a lid. Since you really want to store as much water as you possibly can for you and your family, five gallons is barely enough for a day! In fact, according to figures from the Los Angeles

Department of Water and Power, the average American uses about a hundred gallons of water per day! It's an amazing figure, but true. You probably use way more than you realize when you calculate all your daily usage.

So, how do you store your water without busting your budget? Yes, you can buy large plastic cisterns, glass containers, or ceramic holding tanks, but these will set you back hundreds of dollars. What can you get for next to nothing, or for free?

First, let's look at container materials. The military once used metal cans, which are bulky, heavy, and prone to rust. Metal is not a practical way to store water at your home. Ceramic, clay, and cement are all heavy, bulky, and usually built on-site by do-it-yourselfers.

Then there is glass and plastic. Glass can be obtained free and recycled, and it is the ideal material for water storage because it is inert and the container does not interact with the water inside. But they are breakable and possibly expensive if you must buy them. Instead, wash out and reuse all bottles that you purchase to store water—either rainwater or tap water. You can place them in plastic milk crates to protect them from breaking and securely place sheets of plastic bubble wrap or other packing materials around the bottles. Bubble wrap is easy to obtain for free by saving it when you get it in shipping boxes.

Then there is plastic. Plastic is ubiquitous, and in the food industry, it is constantly discarded. Restaurants, bakeries, grocery stores, caterers, food packers, and commercial kitchens all buy their foods in bulk, often in plastic buckets or tubs or barrels. This includes such products as frosting, dough, oil, pickles, cherries, sugar, etc. A small percentage of these containers are recycled, but most are—sadly—discarded.

If you do a little searching in your area, online, or just the "old-fashioned way"—knocking on doors anywhere they might be used and discarded—you can often find a good source for these five-gallon buckets and larger tubs. Use your imagination and just start asking at likely places; a nearly unlimited volume should be easily obtainable. Just be sure to wash any plastic containers thoroughly before use.

Keep in mind that plastic interacts with its contents, such as water. In fact, ever since things have been packed in plastic, we've all been eating minute amounts of it! That's not a good thing, but you can mollify it slightly by being sure to change out the water in your buckets at least yearly.

RECYCLING HOUSEHOLD WATER

Recycling your household water is good for the environment and saves money as well. You can recycle your kitchen sink water and water from a dishwasher (if you've chosen to keep such an appliance). We use our dishwater three times: first, to wash our dishes; second, to water our window boxes on our deck; and third, as the water drips down to our fruit trees below the deck.

All water from the bathtub and shower can also be discharged into the garden. Water from a washing machine can be diverted into the yard. One of our friends used his washing machine water to water his fragrant roses which grew spectacularly by being fed the water that was enriched by the laundry detergent.

The only water that you would not send into your yard is the water from your toilet.

By the way, I suggest not using a kitchen garbage disposal, and that you remove them. They use too much water. You could compost all those kitchen scraps or feed them to your animals to make those scraps a usable and valuable resource, rather than sending them down into the municipal sewer.

How you go about water recycling depends on where your drainpipes are located and other factors. A house set in a cement foundation is often the most difficult to do recycling because the pipes are not readily accessible.

The nearly ideal situation for recycling water is where one's house is higher on the lot, and the lot slopes downward. That is the arrangement at our non-profit organization, where the building is located on a hilly one-acre site.

Long ago, some of the members of our non-profit went underneath the bathtub, disconnected the drain from the city drain, and connected about 50 feet of discarded galvanized pipe to send all the bathwater down into a lower orchard area. That was easy! At the end of the galvanized pipe, the water can just flow into the orchard. They also added a fitting so a hose can be screwed on. The hose is then moved around to water different parts of the orchard.

Another way to not waste is to use water-absorbing pavers. Install these where you would normally need them, only the water is absorbed into the ground instead of running off into the sewer system or eroding the ground. These can even be used on driveways.

Our washing machine is outdoors, so the drain water is easily diverted to the garden there. And the kitchen sink drain was also disconnected years ago from the urban drain and diverted to trees out beyond the kitchen area.

This reuse of household water makes a lot of sense and has meant a slight reduction in the water bill for watering the extensive plantings around our property.

One must be careful in some cases that the water coming out of the washing machine and the tub are not too hot, though this doesn't seem to have ever been a problem for us.

These pavers allow the water to flow into the soil.

Anyone doing greywater recycling into their own yard must begin to select only those soaps and detergents that contain no unnecessary ingredients (like colors and perfumes) because it's all going to go into your yard where you raise your food! Fortunately, with so much interest in "going green" these days, there are plenty of safe detergents to choose from.

Using an outside sink allows the sink water to flow into the garden.

Julie empties dishwater onto a tree.

Chapter 2
Food

Perhaps if I lived in the rural countryside, I would not think about being ready for emergencies as much as I do. Urban people are used to depending on others, but farmers are used to doing everything themselves, even to a fault. Farmers have long understood that they cannot depend on anyone but family and the next farmer down the road. For example, an apple farmer might have built their own house, fixed their pipes, cleared snow, planted and harvested apple trees, made apple cider, dried and stored apples for winter, made compost, dealt with the outhouse, etc. The day's chore list was long enough that whatever talk goes on in city hall has seemingly little relevance.

> ## IN A NUTSHELL
>
> - Grow food in your existing outdoor space.
> - Learn about edible "weeds."
> - Consider a greenhouse.
> - Support your local farmers market.
> - Never waste food!
> - Make compost.
> - Learn food preservation methods.
> - Buy what you eat and eat what you store!

But I live in Los Angeles, for better or worse! Most people in big cities have the same needs as anyone else anywhere in the world, so it has always made sense for my family and I to do everything we could to be as self-reliant as possible.

One big concern of mine is urban front lawns. They usually measure no more than maybe 40 feet by 20 feet, sometimes bigger, and sometimes smaller. And most folks in residential areas also have backyards. When did growing a grassy lawn become such a standard for that little speck of land? I'm not the first to point this out, but one of the ultimate acts of urban futility is growing useless grass, wasting water and fertilizer and time, then cutting it, and tossing the grass into the trash.

My family uses each piece of land for useful plants, whether for fragrance, food, medicine, or other utility. It's our way of getting more for less. Even beauty is a positive thing, and when we grow roses, they are beautiful, aromatic, and even edible.

I suggest that you use the front yard, side yard, and back yard, whatever yard or outdoor space you have, to grow fruit trees appropriate to your area, vegetables that you like, and herbs that can grow and naturally repel the insects.

This is true permaculture, and you can do as my family does and recycle kitchen and bathwater to feed the fruit trees and other vegetables.

We have done this so long that we couldn't imagine doing anything else. We certainly would not be hiring professional gardeners to mow and blow and keep up an appearance of neatness, self-imposed on some communities, since it's something we eschew.

FOOD PRODUCTION

In just about every case where someone decides to live a more self-reliant life, food production becomes a major focus.

Food production begins with producing the foods that you want to eat and knowing what grows well in your area. As you get good at it, you may produce beyond your own needs, so your excess becomes barter material.

Food production is not just growing trees and crops. It also may include raising bees, chickens, goats, and even larger animals.

When you become a productive member of the permaculture community, even on a small scale, you have created reasons for people to come together—for planting, harvesting, storing, drying, and all the things that it takes for a community to thrive and survive. It should come as no surprise that when a community is actively involved in producing the foods and goods they need, they don't seem to even miss the electronic side of life.

USING YOUR YARD TO GROW FOOD

When I was in middle school, I asked my mother if it would be okay to replace half of our grassy suburban front lawn with a vegetable garden. I am still grateful that she supported the idea. I prepared and plotted out the garden as shown in my gardening books. The garden grew a lot of spectacular, fresh, and delicious foods. We enjoyed zucchini, cucumber, parsley, carrots, corn, and beans—and we marveled at how effective it was—all that summer.

Your outdoor space, even if it's small or in the city, can provide you with food, medicine, and fragrance.

To begin, make a list of all the fruits, vegetables, and herbs that you and your family like to eat. Cross off any that would not grow well in your area. Be sure to add plants native to your area that have the added benefit of food or medicine. After a while, your list will write itself.

Julie planting a vegetable garden in an area that had previously been barren.

A flourishing backyard garden.

Earthworms and compost-loving red wiggler worms (above) are abundant and aerate the rich soil of organic gardens.

Nearly every local area today has a garden club or a neighborhood garden, and this is a good place to talk to other gardeners to learn the timing for planting in your area and what types will and won't work well in your climate. Then, start planting. When is the best time to start planting trees? Ten years ago! So just go ahead and plant your trees.

Visiting nurseries can become overwhelming as you envision all the costs for installment of new edible, medicinal, or otherwise useful landscaping. The costs seem to add up too quickly. That's one reason why so many people put this project off. But where can one find all the resources to get started without spending a lot?

LOW-COST SEEDS AND OTHER SUPPLIES

When you walk around your neighborhood do you see any other neighbors growing foods? If so, these neighbors may want to be part of a seed exchange. Often each participating neighbor has at least a few things they grow. Sometimes they have excesses of produce, as well as excess seeds.

Many neighborhoods have "traditional" foods they grow. If your neighbors are of diverse cultural heritage, you may even find a wealth of new plants to try, such as sweet potato vines used as greens, cactus, chili peppers, pitaya (known also as dragon fruit), and many other "exotic" fruits, as well as North American standbys like strawberries, tomatoes, squash, corn, beans, etc. This is true of the neighborhood gardens in Los Angeles. So, one solution for having a plentiful supply of seeds is to trade seeds. Not only are seeds from vegetables available this way, but also fruit tree seeds, which can grow into fine fruit trees.

Plants that spread and propagate through cuttings can be easily shared when the growing season is at its height. Plants such as strawberries, pitaya, and tree collards growing in your neighbors' yards may be spectacularly overgrown. That is a good time to offer a trade of some kind. Perhaps you have a plant that they would like in exchange. People often need help trimming their fragrant plumeria or grape or berry vines and these cuttings can be rooted and used to start these plants in your own yard. You can also ask if they need certain plant or garden work done in exchange.

Community gardens are another way to find extra seeds and cuttings. Just offer a little time in exchange. Or, in some cases, just being willing to take away the excess is enough payment, and often the gardeners are grateful that you could remove what they would have had to toss into their compost piles. I've found many neighbors are especially happy to receive a valuable plant for their garden, and soon we have a friendship.

Another way to obtain free—or almost free—seeds is through community seed saving groups. Local gardeners have formed alliances to save, promote, and trade seeds from their gardens with other local gardeners. One can join and obtain a few free seed packets of various vegetables per month, usually for a small annual fee. The local group in our area meets monthly to offer members collected seeds at the city library and has a speaker come to talk on gardening topics such as seed saving, sustainability, permaculture, and gardening methods and ecology. There are also Facebook groups where local gardeners swap plants.

It is important to recognize that seeds can change genetically to adapt to the weather and conditions in their local environment in the span of seven generations. Even second-, third-, and fourth-generation plants are much more likely to survive. Therefore, when we obtain seeds grown locally for generations, we also are improving the chances that our plants will grow well.

New gardeners may be surprised to learn that if you plant citrus seeds, you may not get back what you thought you planted. According to Dr. James Bauml, senior botanist at the Los Angeles County Arboretum in Arcadia, California, citrus seeds are polyembryonic, meaning that there can be more than one seedling per seed. Of all the seedlings that sprout from each seed, one will be a sexual (fertilized) embryo, which will not produce the same fruit as the parent. However, the fruits of all the other resulting seedlings will be identical to the parent. So, if two seedlings arise from a seed, one will be the same as the parent, and one won't. If five seedlings arise from a seed, four of the seedlings will be identical to the parent. The percentage of seedlings that will be identical to the parents is a function of how many seedlings eventually sprout from each seed. Your odds are about 50 percent or better of getting the same as the parent when you plant a citrus seed.

Because urban ecology is vulnerable to input from the outside, members of this environment (i.e., city folks) are uniquely vulnerable to disruptions of electricity, water, gas, food, trash pickup, etc. This is why it behooves us to do as much as we can, as individuals, to be food producers and soil-makers. We are "soil-makers" by composting our own kitchen scraps and using earthworm bins for feeding kitchen scraps to worms who turn it into soil. This can even be done by apartment dwellers.

Anyone who wants to start a garden at a low-cost should consider getting manure—a great, usually free fertilizer—from a local small farm or even a stable. First check to see if they use antibiotics or hormones on their animals, as these things may not be desirable to have in your garden. Pet owners who have rabbits or chickens are other good options for free fertilizer. If you offer to help them remove the "garden gold" they may be enthusiastic to help you.

Many people throw away their valuable leaves and other landscaping trimmings, so asking to use these for your garden is often met with strong approval. Likewise many restaurants and stores that serve coffee are often willing to part with their coffee grounds, which would have gone to the trash.

Whenever I hear about rising populations, and strains on the world food supply, I know that it is possible for more and more of us to make the choice to grow food—even a little of our food, in those little places we have. Doing so does more than provide us with food, because when neighbors, friends, and family see it, they sometimes also get inspired to become a part of the solution. They sometimes also choose to become urban farmers.

A raised bed in the narrow space between sidewalk and street.

REVIEW YOUR FOOD SOURCES

- Your garden—whatever foods you grow on your "lawn," in raised beds, out back, fruit trees, etc.
- Neighborhood or community garden
- Local farms
- Farmers markets
- Neighborhood trade network
- Edible weeds
- Foods from street trees

Remember, "food" is everywhere. Your job is to learn to recognize it!

A home garden.

COMMON WILD FOODS

There are many wild foods that are pretty much found nationwide. I encourage you to learn about those wild foods that grow near you and to find ways to incorporate them into your diet.

REMEMBER: Never eat any wild plant until you have accurately identified it as an edible plant. If in doubt, do without! Find ways to take a class, or go on a walk, with a local expert.

Wild nasturtiums bring a salad to life.

Edible cactus grows prolifically, providing food to eat and surplus to barter or sell at farmers markets.

DANDELION
(Taraxacum officinale)

Yes, dandelion is everywhere, and it seems to prefer the urban landscape. Dandelion is frequently despised by gardeners and featured in herbicide ads as a culprit that needs killing. Yet, dandelion is often called poor man's ginseng, a powerhouse of vitamins and minerals available just by eating it. It's a rich source of beta-carotene, even higher than carrots. Since the leaves are bitter, you usually need to cook it or add to soup. Even its roots can be cooked until tender and eaten.

SOW THISTLE
(Sonchus oleraceus)

When most folks see a sow thistle, they think it's a tall dandelion, since the flowers are nearly identical to dandelion. Sow thistle is from Europe, and it grows everywhere. It gets a few feet high typically, with clusters of the yellow dandelion-like flowers. The leaves of sow thistle are tender and palatable uncooked in salads. Sow thistle leaves are also great in stews, egg dishes, soups, etc.

LAMB'S-QUARTER
(Chenopodium album)

Lamb's-quarter is a European native plant that today is found everywhere in the world. It can be found in wilderness areas, but it seems to prefer disturbed soils and back-yards. I've picked it many times from out of the cracks of sidewalks.

The sow thistle plant.

Think of "wild spinach" when you see the lamb's quarter, and the leaves can be used in any recipe where you might use spinach. Great added to salads, the leaves can also be chopped and added to soups, stews, omelets, pasta dishes, stir-fries, etc. This plant is also a close relative to the quinoa seed, so popular today. When lamb's-quarter, an annual plant, matures, it produces a large volume of seeds, which can be harvested and used in all the ways you'd use quinoa. Lamb's-quarter seed is good added to soups, pancake batter, and various grain dishes.

The lamb's-quarter plant.

CHICKWEED
(Stellaria media)

Chickweed is an annual plant from Europe which sprouts up after rain, so you begin to see it in very early spring, and typically it's all dried up and gone by late summer. So you can seasonally enjoy this tender plant in salads. I make salads from chickweed whenever I can, adding dressing,

Chickweed is a low-growing spring plant.

tomatoes, whatever. Yes, you can cook it in soup or with eggs, but it's really best raw. It has tender stems, with a fine line of white hairs along one side of the stem. Leaves are opposite and they come to a tip. There are five deeply cleft petals on each little flower. This tasty edible is so common in lawns and urban gardens that one can purchase an herbicide designed solely to kill chickweed!

STINGING NETTLE
(Urtica dioica)

This plant seems to prefer wet areas, yet it does just as well in backyard urban gardens and little patches of soil downtown. It's from Europe but seems to be just about everywhere in North America. Yes, there's that word "stinging" in its name, and if you brush up against it, lots of tiny hairs release their

Nettles can be found nationwide.

formic acid onto your skin, causing a stinging sensation that might last an hour or so. So, this doesn't go into salad!

But the young tender tops of nettle can be cooked into soups and stews, eliminating the sting, and resulting in a delicious and very nutritious broth. Goes great with many dishes.

PURSLANE
(Portulaca oleraceae)

This plant from India—today found all over the world—is widespread in the urban landscape, typically appearing in summer. It grows flat on the ground with red, round succulent stems and paddle-shaped leaves. The entire above-ground plant is good in salads and many cooked dishes, and it is regarded as the richest plant source of Omega-3 fatty acids. Even Thoreau, at Walden Pond, liked to cook up purslane for his lunch.

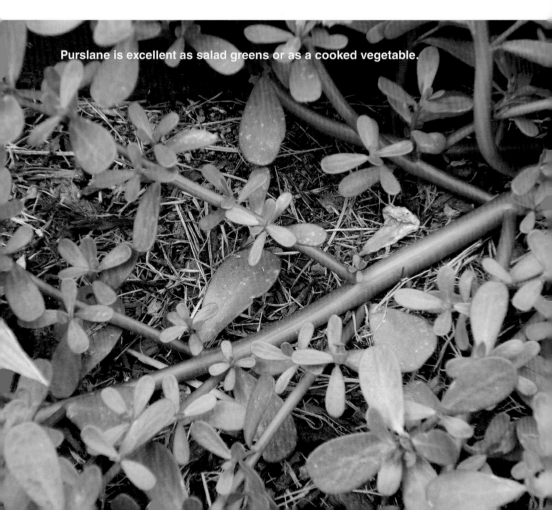

Purslane is excellent as salad greens or as a cooked vegetable.

GREENHOUSES

Greenhouses provide definite benefits for people growing as much of their own food as they can. They also create a more ideal environment for plants to grow in because temperatures vary less and they retain heat or offer shade or cooler temperatures, which means you can supply yourself with fresh vegetables and fruits for more of the year. The main idea is to have a greenhouse that is most appropriate for your area's weather and what you intend to grow. This will extend and possibly improve the growing season. Greenhouses shelter plants from excess cold, heat, and pests.

The warmer temperature in a greenhouse structure occurs because incident solar radiation passes through the transparent roof and walls and is absorbed by the floor, earth, and contents, which become warmer. As the structure is not open to the atmosphere, in colder weather the warmer air cannot escape via convection, therefore the temperature inside the greenhouse rises.

Although today there are highly sophisticated commercial greenhouse systems, a simple DIY set-up can be worthwhile and have many benefits. But before we cover these benefits, it is good to get an idea of your actual needs.

Julie and husband, Talal, in the greenhouse that she built.

Once you've learned what grows well where you live, and you've been experimenting with various food plants, you'll get to the point where you realize the limits of winter farming. This is when you might consider a greenhouse.

These are some of the benefits and advantages of a greenhouse:

- Grow food plants nearly year-round.
- Enjoy lower food bills.
- Have more room for overwintering cold sensitive useful plants.
- Warmer temperatures encourage a larger healthier crop.
- Warmer soil and more steady temperatures promote fertility by causing more seeds to germinate.
- Prevent plant damage from mice, cats, snails, skunks, deer, insects, etc.
- Enjoy gardening in the winter or summer, as it's an ideal shade.
- Add architectural beauty to your garden.
- Add property value to your home.

I have seen a simple greenhouse that was furnished with chandelier and café table! It was very inviting for gatherings with family and friends and it was still a functional greenhouse.

The idea is to create a space to keep the heat in. At the same time, ventilation is one of the important components in a successful greenhouse. The main purpose of ventilation is the regulation of the temperature and humidity at an optimal level, and to ensure movement of air so that plant pathogens do not develop. Ventilation also ensures a supply of fresh air for photosynthesis and plant respiration. The air circulation may enable important pollinators to access the greenhouse crop.

Before you begin to build your greenhouse, of whatever size, consider the ease of entry and egress, since you want that to be convenient. Location, as with most structures, is very important. Consider the orientation to the sun.

BUILDING A LOW-COST GREENHOUSE

Before you spend a lot of money, let's look at some of the ways to create the greenhouse for as little as possible.

To get a jump on the spring planting, many people in farming communities build small low-cost greenhouses for sprouting seeds, using cinder blocks and mostly discarded glass windows. I've found old hefty windows along the side of the street that are great for this method.

Here's how it worked for one such little greenhouse design, which measured perhaps 8 feet wide by about 15 feet long, not huge by greenhouse standards. Cinder blocks were laid out to define the perimeter. On top of this, was a simple framework with two-by-fours, to create a peaked roof, high enough to walk around in. Long glass windows, which

Talal walks among plants elevated on easily made cinderblock-and-pallet tables. These are great, low-cost, durable solutions for greenhouses and outdoor nurseries.

were discarded from some construction project, were placed into the framework. It is easiest to build the two-by-four frame to accommodate the glass windows (not the other way around). A simple door, and inside, some low benches or tables for plantings, complete the greenhouse.

Over the years, I have seen many greenhouses built with discarded windows, and if they are built well, the air temperature inside stays warm and conducive to sprouting seeds even when it's still cold outside. These are one-of-a-kind structures, because their designs are based upon whatever window discards happen to be available.

OTHER FREE OR INEXPENSIVE GREENHOUSE OPTIONS

A simple greenhouse can also be created from the metal framework of a patio canopy or pop-up tent. The metal frameworks of these items are often discarded when the fabric has begun to tear and degrade, and can be found on trash collection days. If you cannot find such a discarded metal framework, it's still fairly easy to fabricate the framework for a greenhouse using two-by-fours or hollow pipes, such as electrical tubing or discarded plastic PVC pipes. These materials are both lightweight and easy to join together.

The ideal framework for a do-it-yourself greenhouse is a rectangular house shape with a peaked roof, since the peaked roof, though not absolutely essential, helps to shed rain and snow during winter. If you have a sufficient volume of piping, you can secure pieces together with bushings, or, if that's not possible, just use duct tape.

Create a simple and convenient door for getting in and out of the greenhouse. Cover the entire structure with light-allowing plastic sheeting. Painter's tarps from the hardware store, the largest size you can find, are relatively cheap, with one millimeter sufficiently thick. Secure seams with clear shipping tape, or duct tape if you prefer.

It will be important to monitor the air temperature inside greenhouses so it doesn't get too hot. For ventilation to regulate temperature, it might work to just keep the door ajar. But, in those cases where this is not practical—or perhaps you have animals that might get into the greenhouse— you will need to create some sort of vent, the easier the better. A vent can be as simple as a flap cut into the top part of the roof, so that the flap can be opened or closed as needed.

Some greenhouses in particularly cold climates have simple fireplaces inside with a vent to the outside. The vent works automatically to reduce heat from the greenhouse, since heat rises, and it will pass through the fireplace to the outside. Also, if it's really cold outside, you could build a small fire in the fireplace for warming the air inside.

QUONSET HUT–STYLE GREENHOUSES

One of the more popular styles of greenhouses on farms and commercial nurseries is the Quonset hut style, which is basically an elongated rectangular floor plan, with an arched roof running the length of the greenhouse.

Tom Nuccio next to the row of Quonset hut–style greenhouses built by a family member for their commercial nursery fifty years earlier.

To create such a greenhouse, all you need are the flexible poles of more-or-less equal length, secured into the ground to create the arch. This can be done with custom-built materials, but I have also observed sturdy greenhouses where this was done with bamboo and old PVC pipes.

To create the framework for the greenhouse, you might have to duct-tape pieces of bamboo together to get the desired length. Remember that you want a greenhouse that allows you to walk in and stand upright, so each of the poles making the arch should be at least about 15 feet long, and probably longer when you consider that at least a foot of each segment of the bamboo will be secured underground. To make sure the framework of a do-it-yourself Quonset hut–style greenhouse is secure, you will also need to secure cross pieces perpendicular to the arches.

Once this is secure to your satisfaction, you can cover it with plastic, add your benches, and your door, and get to work.

One issue with all plastic-covered greenhouses is that the plastic will age and, in some cases, will not stand up to wind. For this reason, if you have this sort of greenhouse—do-it-yourself or a kit—you may need to fix or replace the covering.

SOURCES FOR PRE-MADE GREENHOUSES

Or maybe you just want the greenhouse—now. You don't want to figure out your own construction or source materials. Home garden suppliers will sell anything from a low-cost backyard greenhouse to a top-of-the-line commercial greenhouse, suitable for a serious farming operation. If you just want a kit that you can buy and assemble, here are a few of the possibilities out there.

Peaceful Valley Farm Supply sells a few kits in various price ranges. You can purchase a 6-foot-by-10-foot greenhouse, with framing and cover, for $748. Or you can get a larger greenhouse, with an 8-foot-by-16-foot floor space with redwood framing, for $3,798. You can look at other options at groworganic.com.

World of Greenhouses offers a Weatherguard round-top greenhouse by Jewett Cameron for $949. It measures 12 feet wide, 8'8" tall, and 20 feet deep. It is considered one of the finer greenhouse kits on the market, durable steel tubing and fittings, with a quality poly cover. Check them out at worldofgreenhouses.com.

GrowersSolution.com sells covers for greenhouses, as well as kits to make your own. The prices and sizes vary, so you need to check out their catalog to find something that fits your needs—and pocketbook.

But since our focus here is on "low-cost," we've found that old clear plastic painters' tarps do the job well, as long as you don't mind replacing them every two to three years.

FOOD PRESERVATION

To have food on-hand for emergencies, you can purchase dried, canned, pickled, or freeze-dried foods. In addition, you can do some of your own processing. Let's start with drying.

The Excalibur electric food dryer.

DRYING FOODS

Many foods can be dried and success-fully stored for years. The Excalibur is one of the many food dryers avail-able, which is widely regarded as "the Cadillac" of food dryers.

You can also make your own food dryer. I have several dryers. One is an inexpensive mesh dryer that is used mostly for herbs. Since it gets air cir-culation on all sides, anything put in it dries quickly. Never add foods to this dryer that might attract rats or ants, so use your judgment.

I've also laid sliced fruit and vegeta-bles on screens to dry in the sun. This is very easy to do, but since it might take

A simple open-air mesh food and herb drier.

several days to dry fully, you should cover it at night with cloths to absorb the dew and protect it from birds.

In addition, I use an electric food dryer which cost $25. It's simply a round model, with each layer stackable on the lower layers, and the heat rises through the grid to dry the foods. I use this one for fruits such as persimmons, apples, and pears, and vegetables, acorns, and certain herbs. This is not a sophisticated dryer, but it is very effective at getting the job done.

When the foods are dry, simply pack them in recycled but clean glass or plastic jars. I've used plastic Ziploc bags too, but prefer the glass or plastic jars, usually recycled. I always add a few desiccant packets to the jars to absorb any moisture, and to discourage the hatching of any insects.

PRESERVING FOOD BY PICKLING

This is a basic lesson in pickling from pickling expert Pascal Baudar. Baudar, the author of three books on preservation techniques of wild foods, notes about fifty methods of food preservation, which includes such methods as drying, yeast fermentation, pickling with vinegar or salt, lacto-fermentation, the use of alcohol, and many variations of these.

Lacto-fermentation is a method that preserves foods without modern refrigeration.

In his lesson on lacto-fermentation, Baudar began by dicing wild radish roots, half of a green cabbage, and a handful of greens, including dandelions and wild radish, and put them into a large bowl with two teaspoons of salt per pound of greens. Then he mixed it

Pascal Baudar demonstrates the lacto-fermentation method.

all by hand, which releases the juices of the greens and roots, noting that as "the beginning of a sauerkraut-type ferment."

Baudar explained that in Southern California, where we both live, you should eat such foods within two to three weeks. If it's colder, it will last longer; if it's hot, the fermentation is sped up.

"The food never really goes bad," Baudar said. "But there is a loss of texture of the food, which might be unappealing. If stored in a refrigerator or cold basement, a ferment can last for at least a year."

Lacto-Fermentation Steps

1. Add salt to kill most of the bad bacteria—two teaspoons per pound of food.
2. Introduce sugar, by squeezing the greens (feed the good bacteria).
3. Close the lid to starve the bad bacteria.
4. The food becomes acidic (like vinegar), which is bad for the bad bacteria.

Jars can be kept outdoors in the winter, or in the refrigerator. In warmer climates, if you don't have a refrigerator, the jars should be kept in a basement, or used within two-to-three weeks.

Baudar is original in his use of so many wild foods in his pickling. And because there are so many details to pickling, I strongly recommend his books, especially *Wildcrafted Fermentation: Exploring, Transforming, and Preserving the Wild Flavors of Your Local Terroir*, published in 2020 from Chelsea Green.

BEES

Why keep honeybees?

Will keeping honeybees help improve your self-reliance quotient? Is keeping honeybees a low-cost way to be prepared for emergencies? The answer to both is yes.

You can reduce your costs and improve your health with honeybees. They assist in pollinating your garden and produce honey, pollen, and beeswax.

Selling excess honey is also a good way to make a little extra money. You just need to know how to get started.

Honeybees are tiny in contrast to the work they do. They make up small yet fascinating insect communities. Observing them seems almost like an *Alice in Wonderland*–style "falling down the rabbit hole" experience. What amazing things they do!

Bees are a big concern right now. Bees' impact on agriculture is far greater than most people realize. They are necessary to pollinate fruit trees, almonds, and many other crops that we all depend upon for food.

Julie with her protective bee hood, ready to work on her beehives.

Although bees (like other insects) are self-sufficient, their relationship to us can be beneficial as long as we know what to do to help them. Food and medicine from the hive are wholesome power foods that support health.

Bees naturally make more honey than they can use during the nectar flow season, so the time to harvest honey is once the bees have produced honey exceeding their own needs.

Propolis—the substance bees use to seal hive openings and gaps to prevent intruding parasites—is high in immune

Bee in cactus flower.

system benefits. Wax from unused portions of the beehive can be collected and saved to produce candles, balms, and other useful products.

If interacting with bees is done thoughtfully, it is a beneficial relation-ship. I had a friend who was very interested in bees, but as he got started, he made a few mistakes because he didn't yet know what to do and how to do it, which caused him to get stung too often. As a result, he would panic and that caused the bees to not be at ease with him. He struggled in the same way with dogs, since he was bitten as a child.

Dogs' and bees' animal nature immediately pick up on that fear; in fact, it produces a chemical the bees can "read." Bees, however, will commu-nicate with their sounds if they are uncomfortable, and that gives you an idea of how much interacting at a time can be accomplished in that ses-sion working in the hive.

Our attitude, intent, and actions determine the outcome when working with bees. This is true, in fact for all fauna, all flora, and even human beings!

BEE CARE

Bees need water (they prefer water with algae) and food. In times of the year when naturally occurring food sources are scarce, you can provide food to keep their population strong.

Taking care of bees is similar to gardening, in that there are specific tasks that you need to do at different times of the year. You need to have seasonal planned checks for ridding them of varroa mites, wax moths, and hive beetles, which can be treated effectively by natural treatments, if done on time. The key is to pay attention to be able to act timely when needed!

There are other possible bee diseases. A little research will reveal what is needed. Adjustments need to be made to their hive so that they always have enough room, but not too much. Bees need the correct amount of room in the hive to enable them to resist parasites effectively, keep the correct temperature, and not be overcrowded, which leads to their leav-ing to find a bigger home. They need to be able to raise their broods and store their food.

A mature hive has two lower boxes allowed just for the bees and more boxes are added on for human consumption with a screen between them

Bees feed on painting tray.

which the queen cannot pass called a queen excluder. It prevents the queen from laying her eggs in the upper boxes called supers.

Splitting hives during the seasons when populations increase is one way to increase your apiary or sell the new hives. Catching swarms and removing bees from inauspicious locales are additional possible bee-related beneficial "win-win" endeavors that can be undertaken. You may also able to earn income from these skills.

For me, beekeeping was a new experience, so getting a good idea of how to proceed first was essential to succeeding. Learn more about bees themselves as well as methods for their care. Reading appropriate books, watching videos, and finding a class or mentor are all practical steps to take in preparation for taking on care for bees and the related rewards.

If you choose to husband bees, you can develop your skills, abilities, and character through learning the nuances of their care. Beekeeping does not have to take a lot of your time, but it does take some education and a learning curve to develop familiarity with the processes. After making the effort, you can have healthy hives which produce honey that you can use yourself, sell, or give as gifts. You can also enjoy learning this activity with a friend or family member. This is a wonderful skill to learn and pass down to children, grandchildren, and future generations.

In the very beginning, it may not seem that you are saving money, but you will. And you'll realize that the benefits of keeping bees goes beyond mere money.

BASIC MINIMUM TOOLS & EQUIPMENT FOR BEEKEEPING

Smoker
Every beekeeping supplier sells smokers. These are designed to produce smoke to pacify the bees while you work on the colony. They are an indispensable part of beekeeping.

Boxes and Frames
The bees live in these boxes, with movable frames upon which they build wax and deposit honey.

Hood and Long Gloves
It is impossible to be a beekeeper and never get stung! Of course, you don't want to get stung, but it happens. One of the best and most essential investments when you begin beekeeping is a hood and long gloves through which bees cannot sting.

Other Tools
A brush to gently sweep bees, and a pry bar to lift frames and remove excess wax.

There are other tools, equipment and supplies of the trade as well. I strongly suggest that you locate a local beekeeper or bee organization and learn some of the necessary skills direct from an experienced beekeeper.

I did this, and it helped me tremendously to build my confidence. See recommended books on the subject too.

BASICS OF EMERGENCY STOCKPILE FOOD STORAGE

These are some very basic ideas on food storage that you should be aware of before you start your own food-storage program. In no way is this information all-encompassing; it's meant to provide practical recommendations based on decades of research and experience. Most people cannot go out and pay several thousand dollars—or even several hundred dollars—for a dedicated specialty food storage system. These ideas are to help those on a limited budget get started.

(This section was partly based upon lectures given by WTI member, Ellen Hall, who often encouraged everyone to get started, even on a very limited budget.)

Every commercial prepared-food reserve program requires a sizable initial investment. But there are some relatively inexpensive alternatives. If you provide the leg work and initiative, you can be your own outfitter and avoid much expense.

I also have a deep commitment to nutritional soundness. A British documentary filmmaker related to WTI members his memory of England's food scarcity during World War II. Although bread was plentiful (it was called the "national loaf" and was whole wheat), there was a weekly ration of two ounces of meat and two eggs per person. Though that seemed like a hardship at the time, he learned that post-war research revealed (much to everyone's surprise) that the health of the populace significantly improved during those hard times. Health statistics from that period show reduced incidence of illness (and especially heart disease) than at any other time in England's history. Though other factors doubtless need to be considered, his point was that people can become healthier in times of enforced scarcity if food intake is nutritionally sound.

In support of that, more and more health regimens include a period of outright fasting. If you are adventurous, you might take a month or a week and pretend that there's an emergency national food scarcity. Watch how you and your family survive it as convenience foods disappear, and you're thrown back to basics. As well as learning a great deal about your S.Q. (survival quotient), see if the deprivation adds or subtracts from your overall health and well-being.

PROJECTING COST

If someone had told me, "You need to spend $1,500 per family member per year to store food," I'd never have begun. It is true that many large companies that are in business solely to sell freeze-dried or dehydrated foods quote such figures. Much of this expensive food is marginal in nutritional quality, but there are a few companies that offer a quality line. If cost is no consideration, it may serve you well to contact one of these companies and pay whatever they charge for their convenient service.

But if the excessive cash outlays are out of the question for you, there are alternatives.

A good solid start can be made with just a few hundred dollars, depending on HOW it is done. In fact, if you have NO extra cash, just by stretching your food budget to the limit every month, you can slowly stock up. If you're in that situation, innovate. For example, reduce (or eliminate) restaurant eating for six months or a year. Or buy vegetables that have been reduced in the "for quick sale" shelf at your local grocery store. Or ask vendors at your local farmers market for their fruits and vegetables which are slightly damaged, or too ripe to take back to the farm when they leave the market. These free discards have provided or enhanced many excellent meals for my family.

This abundance of free and discounted foods allows our family to pay less for our weekly fresh foods, which enables us to save money for other aspects of our "food system"—a kitchen device, some equipment, or a new fruit tree now is within reach.

There are many ways to find the money to get started on food storage. Maybe one year you don't take an expensive trip and instead have a "staycation." Or you make all your own birthday presents instead of shopping, etc. Use the money saved to get the rotation process started.

WHERE TO STORE

Preparing a spot to store need not involve a complicated building project. Some cinder blocks or bricks with boards laid on top make adequate shelves that can be erected in a cellar, basement, garage, or even a metal garden shed. The best place is a cellar where the temperature stays cool and steady. In homes that aren't blessed with one of these wonderful, practical storage places, there are some guidelines to follow for choosing a spot to use for storage:

- Store food items close to a wall that receives the least heat (whether from a heater or the sun). Usually, north- or east-facing is best, unless the hotter walls on the west and south are surrounded by shade trees.
- Leave at least one inch between the bottom shelf and the floor, and between the back of the shelves and the wall.
- You can store under beds, in closets, under the house (if dry), even under a table that's draped with a floor-length tablecloth.
- One investment that is well worth the little time and effort to obtain is an indelible ink marker or pen. Attach it to your shelves with a long, sturdy string, then never put anything on the shelf without first marking it with the date.
- I make a list of all the items on my rotation system, and then I place these on my weekly shopping list. This way I can stay on top of the rotation system.

AMOUNTS TO STORE

For a one-year food supply for one person, a basic recommendation follows. You should modify your own list based on your family's eating habits.

- Sugar (some form): 100 pounds
- Salt: 5 pounds
- Wheat (or other whole grains): 300 pounds
- Vitamin A, E, C: daily dose
- Powdered milk: 100 pounds
- Protein powder (e.g., soy): 100 pounds
- Water: 50 gallons

The above is a bare-bones survival ration, even though it may look like a lot. But don't be discouraged, just begin. Do it while supplies are available and affordable.

GRAIN STORAGE

When a person is thoroughly grounded in nutrition, and in the history of famines, one emergency food source emerges as clearly superior to all others: whole grains. Whether the grain is wheat, rice, corn, millet, etc., the key is that you store the whole grain. As a sustaining food for mankind, grains are time-tested. They have been the major staple of the human diet since our species made the basic shift from nomad hunter-gatherer to cultivator.

Ellen Hall's family chose to focus on wheat since it was the most familiar and readily available. She used it to make breads, pancakes, and cereals. She chose rice as a backup and looked on it as a supplemental staple. Wheat stores better and longer than rice for two reasons. The oil in the rice kernel is slightly more perishable, and rice has a softer shell. White rice stores better, but it is far less nutritious. We have also used barley, buckwheat, quinoa, and chia seeds as regular staple grains.

CONTAINERS

Three five-gallon buckets will hold approximately 100 pounds of wheat or rice. Be sure you are getting "food grade" buckets. An airtight seal is essential. Even minute amounts of oxygen seeping into the grain leads almost certainly to insect infestation. And escaping grain odors may attract rodents, some of which can eat through plastic. If sourcing is a difficulty, check with the nearest LDS (Mormon) Church—they are usually able to refer you to a local source of high-quality tubs or buckets for long-term food storage.

DRY ICE

Desiccant packages are readily obtainable and just as reliable as the dry ice method described below. But make sure that these, too, are food-grade. If you choose to follow the dry ice method, dry ice can be obtained from some markets, fire extinguisher supply companies or RV/camping supply stores. Or just go online to find the nearest source in your neighborhood.

PUTTING IT ALL TOGETHER

1. Pour the whole grain of your choice into five-gallon buckets.
2. Place a two-inch square chunk of dry ice (broken off with a hammer or screwdriver) on top of the grain in each bucket.
3. Lay the loose lids on top of the buckets. Do not seal. Wait at least 12 hours.
4. After the dry ice completely evaporates, press the lids onto the buckets so that they seal.

As dry ice evaporates, carbon dioxide gas is emitted, displacing the oxygen surrounding the grains. Carbon dioxide gas is heavier than oxygen, so it drifts down to the bottom of the bucket. In effect, this "pushes out" the oxygen that bugs that usually infest grains live on.

Caution: Guard against moisture that will form if you seal the lid before the dry ice has totally evaporated.

If the dry ice has not evaporated before the lid has sealed, it may cause a mild explosion from the expanding carbon dioxide gas. Though this would prove to be messy, it's not really dangerous.

Twelve hours is the minimum time to wait before sealing the containers.

Again, most people now store grains using packages of food-grade desiccants, but the dry ice method is still useful and effective.

BEANS

Beans ensure that there's a balanced protein with the staple grains. Beans are especially high in an amino acid called lysine, and

Julie packs beans with desiccant packages.

when they're eaten along with wheat or corn (which are low in lysine), the amount of protein the human body can use is increased 30 to 40 percent.

I purchase pinto beans; I find that they store very well in airtight metal tins with no dry ice treatment. Most varieties become increasingly dry upon long storage and require longer cooking time.

NUTS

If you make a trip to the wholesale produce market in the fall when the new crop has arrived, the prices are very good on large quantities of nuts. My family buys enough for the whole year. Nuts have a high oil content and therefore a relatively short shelf life, unless they are vacuum-packed or all of the oxygen is removed from the container in which they are stored.

But shelled walnuts, for example, can be preserved with the following method: Pack dry in sterilized jars and seal the jars tightly. Then place the jars in the oven and bake at 275 degrees Fahrenheit for an hour. Give the tops of the jars an extra tight twist after removing from the oven. The walnuts will keep, with this processing, up to five years.

SEEDS

Dried green peas, lentils, and corn all store well, and should be considered for your stockpile according to your family's taste. But seeds for sprouting are essential to any food storage program. In a widespread emergency, any foods formerly purchased fresh every few days will be a luxury of the past. All nutritional benefits that are derived from a fresh green salad can be acquired through seed sprouts; in fact, some sprouts are much more nutritious than lettuce. I've settled upon alfalfa seeds, chia seeds, and mung beans for sprouting. In nearly a decade of use, I've never found any of them to be bug-infested or to fail to sprout.

Because sprouts grow so easily, they're an especially delightful task for children to take charge of.

SUGARS

The best quality sugars that are whole foods and aren't devoid of nutrients are in liquid forms such as honey, agave, sorghum, or various types of molasses (sugar cane, carob, et al.). Honey is the best "sugar" I've found. Five-pound cans of honey store indefinitely and occasionally go on sale. Also, honey-packing houses will sometimes sell dented cans for a discount. Older honey will crystallize, but it will easily melt when gently heated.

With several hives now on our property, I am assured of a relatively stable source of a top quality "sugar."

A beekeeper inspects a frame in his hive.

POWDERED MILK

Dried powdered milk (non-instant) lasts up to 60 months at 40 degrees Fahrenheit, but only 24 months at 70 degrees Fahrenheit. Thus, relative to grains, it does not store very well. Keep a supply in your refrigerator or freezer, as homemade baked goods are undoubtedly vastly improved in texture and sweetness by the addition of powdered milk. As it is virtually impossible for an individual to prepare dried milk for long-term storage, the commercially prepared (albeit more expensive) product is worth the expense.

Powdered milk is great in your food storage plans. It allows you to have milk even without refrigeration, plus you can save money by buying powdered milk.

There are two different types of powdered milk: instant and non-instant. Both powdered types of milk have the same texture and versatility. With both, you can make milk that you can drink, cook with, and make yogurt. The nutritional value is the same in both, since they are both made from non-fat milk.

Instant is best used for "drinking" milk. Things you need to know about instant powdered milk:

- It is lightweight, more so than the non-instant.
- It is "fluffy," which means it takes up more space on your shelves.

- It dissolves quickly into cold water to drink.
- It's usually more expensive than non-instant.
- It tastes more like "regular" milk from a jug.

Non-instant milk is a little bit harder to find, and while you can drink it, it typically is used for cooking. Here are some things you need to know about non-instant powdered milk:

- It is slightly heavier and cheaper than instant milk.
- It's best to dissolve in warm water using a blender or whisk.

Instant and non-instant powdered milk may both come in number 10-sized cans. Such a quantity of instant will only make about two gallons of milk. By contrast, the same quantity of non-instant will make about three-and-a-half gallons. So look closely at the pricing.

GRAIN COMPANIONS

If you chose wheat, for example, as your staple, you will need to consider what other products you'll need to use it effectively. For example, leavening agents are useful for causing baked goods to puff up with air. One leavening agent—yeast—is alive, but it doesn't stay alive more than four to six months (at room temperature). Although some people claim fair success at freezing yeast, it seems to call for an active rotation system.

Baking powder will work for leavening "quick bread" or pan bread; it stays active up to four years. And then there's perhaps the best solution to the leavening question: keep a sourdough starter. Besides lasting indefinitely, many people agree that nothing tastes better than whole-wheat sourdough homemade bread, fresh out of the oven.

SALT

A top-quality sea salt purchased in quantity will be surprisingly inexpensive. The only storage requirement is to keep it dry.

CONDIMENTS

List which spices you use regularly, and stock up. In addition, soy sauce, dried "natural" soups, and bouillon cubes (and the like) will help to make your grains taste delicious and provide variety.

MEAT

One friend of mine said, "If I had to live on rice, I'd die anyway, so why bother?" The most valuable information I've found on the subject of meat and meat substitutes was in *Diet for a Small Planet* by Frances Moore Lappé. No publication on the subject is more recommended, because not only does it provide answers about balancing protein intake with grains, but it also gives recipes that include the per-ounce protein equivalent to steak.

COFFEE

If you have become accustomed to a stimulant, such as coffee or tea, a survival situation is rough enough without going through withdrawal symptoms. Either give it up now or stock up on it.

CANNED FOODS

Buy in case lots and mark each can with the date of purchase when you get home.

Begin to rotate for freshness by placing newly bought cans at the back of the case and using the cans up front first. This way you always have a full case of safe, "fresh" food.

Thoughtful shopping is really the answer to most questions about food storage. For example, in the fall, when the apple crop comes in, fresh apple prices will drop. Keep watching; when apple prices go down, apple juice prices drop dramatically, as do prices for applesauce, apple butter, apple cider, apple pie filling. This is the time to buy in bulk—get a case or two.

This way of going about preparing the household is not panic hoarding—this is sound purchase policy. It is utterly natural to stock in a supply of apples or tomatoes when they are in season. What is unnatural, in fact, is the enormous amount of time, gasoline, and money most of us spend on incessant trips to the store—sometimes for every meal.

When deciding what canned goods to buy, the first consideration is to purchase only those that you use regularly. In other words, what you don't eat now, you'll likely not enjoy eating even in an emergency.

Some foods that my family buys in bulk and rotates include olives, dill pickles, whole kernel corn, nuts, pickled jalapeños, canned beans, tofu, stuffed grape leaves, chili salsa, fruit packed in its own juice, etc.

Think and plan before you buy. Case in point: A friend who became caught up in the "stocking up" idea rushed to stock her cellar but didn't plan for rotating or using the canned goods. They remained in her cellar for a decade. My colleagues convinced this friend to begin opening items for testing. Now she is using the good stock and steadily replacing everything with fresh purchases.

(Interestingly, eight of us have participated in testing this canned food, some of which was over ten years old. We really take our hats off to the American food-processing industry: Everything—so far—has been tasty, colorful, and not a bit "off" in any way.)

DEHYDRATED FOODS

The shelf-life of dried foods is about six months to a year, requiring no refrigeration. Fruits, meats, and vegetables can be dehydrated at home with any of the purpose-made food dehydrators sold today. It is also possible to build your own. (See section on Drying Foods, earlier in this chapter.)

The supermarket variety of dried fruits have often been treated chemically to retain color and flavor, and resist infestation. But dried fruits are available without preservative chemicals such as sulfur dioxide, which causes negative reaction with some people. So be sure to read labels and ask questions.

If you decide to depend on dehydrated foods in your emergency storage, be sure to check with the manufacturer to determine how they process their food.

FREEZE-DRIED FOODS

Freeze-dried foods are flash-frozen to very low temperatures and then dried while still frozen. They are more expensive than dehydrated (sometimes double the cost) but have the following comparative advantages:

- They're usually additive free.
- They can be reconstituted much more rapidly.
- They require no cooking which may be an important consideration in an emergency.
- There is a wider variety of fruits available.

Although some speak of freeze-drying as a relatively new technology, it was used hundreds of years ago by the Incas to preserve food high in the Andes. They embraced the frosty nights at 12,000-foot elevation as an asset and freeze-dried some of their harvest. In lean years, they always had stores of freeze-dried ducks and potatoes. The success of this civilization has been attributed to their careful administration of food supplies.

The nutritional value of foods that are dehydrated or freeze-dried depends on many variables in processing: What quality of food was used to begin with? What chemicals were used? What temperatures? Duration of treatment? How was it packaged?

There's really a lot to know. Always seek the most reliable sources that seem most committed to top-quality food.

Above all, "Eat what you store; store what you eat" is the basic principle that should guide all your food-storage buying.

To Plant A Garden
Is to Believe In The Future

CHAPTER 3
Cooking

Outdoor kitchen set-up.

In case a disaster, emergency, or other disruption occurs that prevents you from cooking in your indoor kitchen, you should have the means and the ability to cook a meal outdoors.

In order to do this somewhat easily and efficiently, you need a table or other surface (though not essential), a stove (more than one is even better), and whatever fuel you need for the stove.

My family keeps a little table out back where we place our portable outdoor stove. We can cook a meal as quickly there as we can indoors. We use our outdoor set-up every now and again not just to keep in practice, but because we enjoy cooking outside where we can hear the birds and feel the sun and the breeze. Plus, this keeps the house cooler in summer.

The portable stove, or camping stove, is perhaps our easiest stove to use, because it operates very much like an indoor range. It looks like a briefcase, which you open to reveal the stove. Some similar stoves even have collapsible legs—no table needed. You screw on a bottle of liquid fuel (propane), which must be purchased and stored for whenever it's needed.

I use my outdoor stove to cook lots of meals, such as vegetable dishes full of greens from the yard. As a practical matter, I keep a little tray handy with olive oil for the pan, a spatula, and a large cast iron skillet. Everything that you need for basic cooking should be easily carried on a small tray.

Everyone reading this should be able to cook in the backyard with little stoves like this and/or hibachis. The hibachi is even more basic, and though they come in different sizes, most basic models are about a foot square, suitable for one pan or pot. They usually rely upon charcoal as fuel, though we have used dried twigs to cook meals as well. This means that you need to keep a source of firewood and twigs, and you need to start your fire and reduce it to coals before you're ready to cook.

IN A NUTSHELL

- Set up an outdoor kitchen
- Identify multiple outdoor cooking methods and fuel sources
- Make practicing outdoor cooking a monthly habit

Just having a camping stove and having fuel stored is okay, but usually not enough for an emergency scenario. You want to stay in practice, testing your supplies periodically so that if you had no other choice, it would be an easy transition. Remember, the hardest part for many people during emergencies is the psychological hurdle. Practicing readiness skills makes this less difficult and more enjoyable.

One of the reasons some people don't want to cook outdoors is because they think it's dirty, or that bugs will get into the food, or because they are worried about what the neighbors might think. I think the "dirty" reason is the biggest for most people, but the clean-

A homemade rocket stove.

liness of your cooking area is entirely under your control. Just keep a table area clear and clean and keep your supplies handy in a box. Though I do keep some supplies outdoors in a covered container, most of the time I just grab a few staples from my kitchen before I go outdoors to cook. I try to keep it as simple and uncomplicated as possible.

Many people regularly use gas or charcoal barbecue grills, as well as indoor woodstoves that were relegated to the yard. A simple grill is probably already in your yard, and I have obtained grills left for trash pickup that had no problems at all. I once asked a man why he was discarding his barbecue (which I took), and he said there was nothing wrong with it, but he had recently purchased a new larger model. Typically, people use charcoal in the barbecue, but I usually use twigs and small branches.

People occasionally get rid of an old wood stove, either when upgrading or because they no longer want it. I've also seen old woodstoves in the

A simple cement block "stove."

trash on garbage pick-up day, and I've seen them in flea markets and thrift stores. This is more common in rural areas.

A cast-iron woodstove left outdoors will often need to be treated to reduce rust. I recommend painting periodically with high-heat engine paint and or covering it with a weather-resisting cover and placing the feet or corners on bricks to keep it off the ground. Still, I've seen and used outdoor woodstoves that were outside for a few decades, and they still worked fine.

Cooking on a wood stove takes a bit of practice because the body of the woodstove, where the fire burns, is typically relatively large, and not directly under the pot or skillet. So you need to build up a good fire,

An outdoor wood stove.

and then cook on those flames, or you build up a fire and let it burn until there is sufficient heat to cook food on the top of the stove.

You probably never need to buy firewood if you keep your eyes open. Wood is commonly discarded in cities when people prune their trees and shrubs, and it is obviously extremely common in the rural areas. Just save your tree and shrub prunings, cut them to size, and use them when dry.

And then, you can complete the ecological cycle. When you clean out the fireplace or woodstove, sprinkle those ashes in your garden and around your trees. The ash provides valuable nutrients to your plants.

A woodpile cut mostly from pruned wood on the property.

SOLAR COOKING

By now, just about everyone has heard about solar cookers of one sort or another. And you know an idea has finally gone "mainstream" when you open a glossy mail-order catalog and find solar cookers for sale. Nevertheless, most residents of the United States still think of solar cookers as a sort of novelty—perhaps a good weekend project for Scouts, but

The very efficient SunOven.

Prudence (left) demonstrates the use of the SunOven at a farmers market.

not something that is practical and useful. This viewpoint is unfortunate. In part, this attitude results from the high cost of prefab solar cookers—some cost several hundred dollars! Plus, many people believe that their yard doesn't get enough sun to make solar cookers practical.

In fact, solar cookers are practical just about everywhere in the United States for at least six to eight months every year. As for cost, you could purchase a used prefab solar cooker, or buy on sale if the full retail price is too much. Or you could just make your own.

Julie cooks outdoors on a SunOven.

HOW TO MAKE A LOW-COST SOLAR OVEN

Many readers of *Mother Earth News* have made their own solar cookers using directions described in past issues, particularly the parabolic dish solar cooker, and the "bread box" design made from wood or sheet metal. If you want to make your own solar oven from scratch, you can start with a very simple low-cost solar cooker that can be made for $10 or so. Using the "Box-In-A-Box" design, a simple solar cooker can be made with cardboard boxes.

Nhan Esteban cooks on a parabolic solar cooker.

First, get two cardboard boxes. One should be able to fit into the other, with ideally an inch of space between them all around. (If you can't find boxes, you can create your own boxes from cardboard pieces and sturdy tape.) Cover the inside of the smaller box with aluminum foil, and make sure that you tape down any loose flaps on either box.

After placing the smaller box into the bigger box, the tops of each box should be at the same level. To accomplish this you may need to support the inner box so that it is off the floor of the bigger box. You can insert four small pieces of wood to serve as four "legs" to support the inner box. Or you can use several pieces of cardboard to raise up the inner box, or small empty cans (such as those from tuna or cat food).

Once you've placed and glued these "legs," pack all the space between the two boxes with crumpled newspapers or other insulation; you could also use old cotton rags, straw, dried grass, coconut fiber, etc. Though you might be tempted to use those white blown-foam packing chips for insulation, don't! At high temperatures, they may melt and/or give off undesirable fumes.

Now that you have one box inside another, with both of their tops level, and with the insulation packed between the boxes, you are ready to seal the insulation. This is done simply by taping (or gluing pieces of cardboard) over the top open section between the two boxes. I generally just use duct tape.

Next, make a lid for your cooker. If you were lucky enough to find a large cardboard box with a tight-fitting lid, you can just use that lid. If not, you may need to cut a lid from cardboard. To do this, measure the size of the big box, and then cut your cardboard at least one inch larger on all sides. This is so you can fold down the edges and have a flap to your lid.

Once you have made your secure-fitting lid, you are ready to cut an opening for a sheet of glass.

Up to this point, you could have constructed everything from old boxes and from supplies you have around the house.

You now want to cut an flap in the lid that is just as big as the opening of the inner box. Try to cut the opening only on three sides. It will function as a reflector for the final oven.

The new opening of the lid will need to be covered with a single pane of glass, or with a sheet of clear plastic. Plastic might be easier to obtain, but glass will retain the heat better. The glass or plastic must be secured to the top of the lid by glue, silicone caulking, or duct tape. Make certain that the glass is secure before proceeding.

Line the inside of the lid flap with aluminum foil, and you have a reflector. When the solar cooker is in use, you prop up the reflector with a stick.

Presto! Your solar cooker is complete.

By carefully planning before you begin the actual work, you will produce a quality cooker with minimal effort. For example, rather than rotely follow these directions, first see what sort of supplies you already have at hand. You may have a good pane of glass, and so you should adjust the cooker's size based upon the glass. Or you may find two ideal cardboard boxes, and so you adjust all sizes accordingly.

Before you cook, place a metal cookie tray, or an aluminum foil tray, on the inside of the cooker.

Once it's built, using the solar cooker is easy. To best absorb the heat, all cooking pots should be black and should be covered. Food placed inside will cook faster if it is cut into smaller pieces. But you should always allow twice as much cooking time in a solar cooker.

The solar cooker is one of the simplest ways to cook, and it forces you to plan your meals in advance.

BUILDING A "BOX-IN-A-BOX" SOLAR OVEN

The supplies needed to make a low-cost DIY solar oven.

Step 1: Make sure the smaller box fits into the larger box with a few inches all around.

Step 2: Line the inner box with aluminum foil.

(The finished inner box should look like this.)

Step 3: Add spacers inside the larger box prevent the smaller box from compacting the insulation between the two boxes.

Step 4: Add wadded newspaper into the larger box for insulation.

Step 5: Seal the space between the two boxes.

Step 6: Secure the seal between the two boxes using duct tape.

Step 7: Make the cover for the solar cooker by cutting an opening in the larger box lid. Be sure to only cut the opening on three sides and line the oven-side with foil.

Step 8: Fix a sheet of glass to the opening of the lid using duct tape.

Now finished, the cooker can be used.

A stick holds up the reflector lid as the beans inside cook.

Chapter 4

Power Sources

We've all grown accustomed to electricity in our lives. Some say we're addicted. Life as we know it would cease to exist without the steady flow of electrons. But most of us have so acclimated our lives to the availability of electricity that it's hard to imagine life without it. We flip the switch, and we have light, or a TV, radio, computer. Modern banking would not exist without electricity, nor would most communication.

Fortunately many inroads have been made to decentralize electricity, at least for those who choose to educate themselves and get off the grid, a little or a lot. This means some of us will still have ways to access power if the whole grid goes down.

Journalist Ted Koppel's 2015 bestseller *Lights Out* explored the feasibility of a cyberattack or other terrorist act to take down essentially three power grids in the United States. Though he points out that this would not be easy, it could be done and—perhaps to the dismay of the reader—there is no meaningful action plan to deal with such an eventuality.

I have no crystal ball, but it's important to plan for any eventuality. Let's just look at life without electricity and explore the ways in which we would live without it. More immediately, for those who wish to live better on less, you might find ways to save money by using less electricity even while you have unlimited access.

THE TRANSITION

If electricity were to go out, broadly and suddenly, the results would be disastrous. But a prepared person would be better able to survive.

First, there would be widespread panic because most means of communication—except word of mouth—would be eliminated. The lack of communication means much more than not knowing what happened. It means that whatever method you've relied upon to communicate with your family, friends, students, fellow workers, etc., will be gone.

In the interim, battery-powered walkie-talkies could be of some help. But we will all suddenly and painfully learn that we overly relied on technology and have scant few alternatives.

Bells and other sounding devices could be used for communications, as could fires on hilltops, but these systems would take time to develop. I can visualize a brisk business in bicycle couriers for hand-delivered notes.

You should always discuss the day's plans with family members and discuss action plans and where to gather in the event of an emergency.

While it is unlikely that we would see a quick and rapid descent of a society into a stone age, the more you can do for yourself and your community, the more prepared you will be.

When you buy tools and gear, always consider your ability to get work done without electricity. Electric drills are quick and convenient, but hand-cranked drills are easy to come by and do the job in almost the same amount of time. For the kitchen, there are hand-cranked components to coffee grinders, juicers, food processors, etc.

Most home tasks can be done without electricity, with minimal adjustment. In the average household, perhaps the two appliances that would be hard to replace would be the refrigerator and the washing machine.

We'll discuss in the Hygiene chapter that you can always wash your clothes by hand. That's what everyone did before electricity. You can check out the stores where the Amish purchase their goods and find various devices for washing clothes. Our "solar clothes dryer" is just the old-fashioned clothesline!

Refrigerators that are 12VDC are available at recreational vehicle suppliers but are not in wide use. Still, you could obtain such a refrigerator and power it indefinitely with a few solar panels.

Otherwise, without refrigeration, food would spoil quickly, and everyone would need to start drying or pickling foods immediately. Those who have already been involved in home food storage would be well ahead of the game since they already know some of the basics. (We discussed the importance of having a garden and storing food without a refrigerator in the Food chapter.)

LIVING WITHOUT ELECTRICITY

Though it's possible to live without electricity, not many choose to do so in the urban environments largely because the city is not set up for us to live self-reliantly.

This means that if you choose to live without electricity, and more self-reliantly, you must find the ways to do so within your limitations. Or you need to move to a more rural environment where it will be much simpler to do so.

To live ecologically and without electricity does not necessarily mean to live without technologies. In the United States, the best example of people

Amish buggies in rural Ohio.

choosing to live without electricity are the Amish, who reside mostly in rural Ohio and Pennsylvania on large family farms.

I'll discuss some of the ways to apply the Amish example to the typical American lifestyle. For example, there are several companies that cater almost exclusively to the Amish and their needs, but anyone can purchase from these companies. Lehmans.com is one such source of kitchen and farm appliances that are hand-operated.

HOUSING

First, the Amish know a thing or two about house and barn building and how to keep costs down. How do they do it? When the Bylers need a new barn, everyone in the county gets together and works on the barn until it's done. The house is then over-built, well-insulated, and situated to take advantage of the sun, winds, and even the flow of seasonal streams. A house well-positioned and properly built can use 85 percent less fuel to heat and cool it.

HEATING AND COOLING

Heating and cooling the modern home is one of the biggest expenses of the modern American household. The Amish build their homes facing the south to take advantage of the sun (remember, they have no electric lighting). The north roof is typically sloped more steeply so the snow slides off. The windows are always double-paned to hold in the heat from wood stoves, and the walls are far more insulated than the average American home.

But there is no reason why every house built cannot have thicker walls and insulated walls, floors, and ceilings. It's the easiest and most cost-effective way to create homes that will use far less energy over their lifetime for heating and cooling. It is typically not done because this can add several thousand dollars to construction costs. The building trade—and house-flipping mania—is more concerned about turning a quick buck. So it's up to the individual homeowner to make sure their home is properly insulated. Insulation and thick walls are the best single investment you can make to reduce heating and cooling costs.

In order to not require electricity to cool the home in summer and heat the home in winter, you can use a variety of passive methods and a few low-tech methods.

A solar-operated attic fan can help to draw the heat out of the attic or roof in the summer and keep the house cooler. Another passive option is to have the ability to have a cross-breeze through the house. Doing this is largely dependent on the local wind conditions and orientation of the house.

WOOD STOVES

Though some Amish have fireplaces, most have wood stoves used both for cooking and heating. Some urban communities have banned wood stoves and fireplaces, giving the reasoning that the smoke contributes to bad air quality. (See, it is accurate that cities can work against your being self-reliant.) Still, you should investigate quality wood stoves for both heating and cooking.

Using a wood stove can dramatically improve your ability to live self-reliantly. There are many companies that still manufacture these, but these stoves are widely available second-hand. How do you know if the stove is still good? Just examine it carefully. Is there rust that threatens the integrity of any of the walls? Does the door work easily? Are there any missing parts? Are the venting pipes included?

Once you purchase one, be sure to properly install it. You want to enjoy your woodstove indoors, not outdoors watching as your house burns down. Also, remember that you want a regular source of wood, ideally one that you do not need to pay for.

LIGHTING

Electric lighting is a big part of any modern home, but with proper construction and aligning the most-used rooms of the house to the south, you can minimize the need for electricity during the day. There are also light tubes that bring the daytime light into the inside of the home quite effectively. Today, these are available at all big box building supply stores.

Light tubes are an excellent way to have quality lighting indoors during the day without the use of electricity. Some include batteries that store power so that you'll also have the possibility of "solar lighting" at night.

Additionally, there are all manner of oil lamps that produce lighting nearly as good as electric lighting.

And if you chose to be totally off the grid with no wiring, you still might like some battery-operated lanterns, which are readily available. You can purchase modern rechargeable batteries and recharge them in one of the solar rechargers currently available.

Light tubes.

Solar battery charger.

Don't forget candles. We see them at flea markets, yard sales, and thrift stores for next to nothing, because most people don't appreciate the value of candles—until the power goes out.

REFRIGERATION

In many parts of the world where there is no electric refrigeration, people purchase dried goods and canned goods, and simply go to local farmers markets to purchase fresh produce.

Until about the 1950s, people used to have regular home delivery of fresh milk! And most homes would have a cooler cabinet somewhere in the kitchen. The shelves are all heavy-duty screen and the cabinet is open all the way from the basement to the attic. This allows an air flow, and it keeps foods cooler than if they were just out in the open or in a closed cupboard.

Ice boxes are things of the past, but in the pre-electricity days, people owned a heavily insulated cabinet, and they would put ice onto the top of it. The cold air descends, so the cooling effect would keep the food inside the cabinet cooler. You can still buy ice boxes at antique shops, but you'd need to have a supply of ice, and the most practical way to have a steady supply of ice is through modern refrigeration, so that's why most off-the-grid folks don't have one of these.

With no electric refrigeration, all your food will be canned, home-canned, dried (like rice, beans, pasta, dried fruits and vegetables, dried meats, etc.), freeze-dried, or in retort bags. You can also keep a garden going, constantly grow some of your food, and learn the wild foods you can harvest. Also, get to know all your local farms.

Our friend in Los Angeles, Chanel-Patricia, did not want an electric refrigerator. So she purchased everything dried or canned and often went to her local market, located just one block away. For those items that absolutely needed to be kept cool, she had a makeshift evaporative cooler on her kitchen counter. She simply placed the items into what looked like a large dish pan, added some water, and draped a cotton cloth entirely over the food items.

This simple evaporative cooler is simply a dish pan with water. The contents—such as milk, cottage cheese, butter, etc.—are covered with a cotton cloth.

The water was slowly drawn into the cotton and evaporated, and this kept the food cool enough for the few days before it was consumed.

MANUAL TOOLS

For most of the myriad tasks where you would employ an electric appliance, you can still use a manual device. Someone choosing to eschew electricity would need to buy manual tools. This would include such things as manual coffee grinders, manual juicer, manual can opener, etc. You can also buy manual drills, saws, rasps, and so on.

A manual coffee grinder.

PHONES AND OTHER ELECTRONICS

You could probably have a cellphone with no home wiring, assuming you had cell coverage where you lived. You'd just need to have a small solar charger that you plugged your phone into during the day when it needed charging.

Television? Many people pursuing a non-electric lifestyle do not want a television. However, there are valuable lessons to share with family and friends in some programs on the "far-seeing magic lantern," as Richard E. White calls it. Of course, much of what is on television is debasing and full of negative role-modeling. But there are also programs that can help you to survive physically, mentally, morally, and spiritually. These have vital lessons. These include special movies, documentaries, newscasts, instructional and arts programs, and more.

Through the RV industry, there is an endless array of electric devices powered on 12 volts DC. Conceivably, perhaps as a compromise, you could have a small TV and run it from batteries powered from the sun. You'd still be off grid.

The computer is inherently an electrical device, so you'd need electricity from batteries or a solar source, somehow, if you wanted or needed a computer. But remember, you can get news from a newspaper or radio. In fact, it has been argued that most of us who have all the facts in the world at our fingertips with our smartphones are no better informed than people who read and study carefully. Some sociologists have observed that though the average smartphone user can easily access facts, the ability to understand the deeper meaning of historical events, ongoing politics, and even controversial facts, is now more garbled than ever because so many want instant gratification without doing the intense work that is required. The result, hard as it is for many to accept, is that computers and smartphones, despite their obvious benefits, may have had the unintended consequence of dumbing us down.

No wonder there are those who have simply continued with their lives, without smartphones or computers. The continuance of life does not require these devices, and those who have chosen to leave them alone may very well have rich and fulfilling lives.

THE SOLAR SOLUTION

Utilizing solar power is a cost-effective, logical solution to those electric power needs essential to everyday life in our society and homes. Solar power can greatly improve life during emergency situations by powering lights, charging electronics, and providing energy for a large range of devices. It provides not only low-cost advantages of renewable free energy, but it also enables us to contribute to solutions for our planet.

Gasoline, which our economy is addicted to, is expensive, even more so during times of war or unrest. This addiction has been and continues to be the root cause of many people being killed and lives torn apart in wars around the globe. Supporting the fossil fuel model is costly to our health, our integrity, and with a bigger view, our planetary home. Using our solar alternatives remedies reliance on polluting gas and oil fuels. Energy from coal and nuclear sources can and should be reduced and replaced by already developed and available technology.

SOLAR ENERGY: HOW BRIGHT IS THE FUTURE?

by Talal Balaa

The author was head of a sustainability unit at a large school district with an energy budget over $125 million, overseeing multiple solar installations and a large program of innovative and emerging technology. Balaa is NABCEP-certified and a licensed professional engineer.

This guest chapter will answer these questions:
- What is solar energy?
- What hurdles can be in your way when you try to install it?
- We will also address the costs, the benefits, and how the use of solar energy helps resiliency.
- Lastly, we will consider the downsides to using solar, and wrap up with the available resources that can help us make better choices.

Types of Solar Energy
The solar panels you see on the roofs of houses, and in some cases, in large installations, are photovoltaic (PV). But solar energy can be

harnessed in many other ways. For example, the heat from the sun can help keep a home warm in winter—that's passive solar. One example is Trombe walls, a very thick wall facing south that can store store heat in the winter, while being shaded in the summer.

A Trombe wall in Cheyenne, Wyoming.

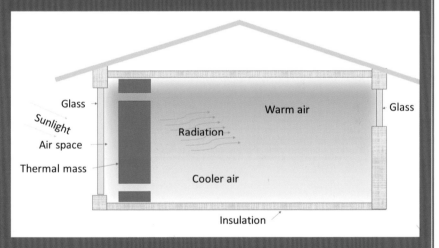

How the Trombe wall works.

Solar energy can also be used to purify water, as with a solar still. You can also do concentrated solar and heat water to produce steam. That steam can be used in a traditional turbine-based generator. And you have already learned about solar ovens in the Food chapter.

There are applications where solar energy, or solar and wind energy, is used to create ice, which is then used for cooling.

Solar Energy Hurdles

What are the hurdles to installing solar? First, although solar panels have become more and more efficient, you need a relatively large roof area. Your roof must be in good condition. For an average home, you may need about 20 photovoltaic panels, and each is about 10 square feet, which will typically occupy half the roof.

Next, think about trees or buildings that might shade your proposed panels. That can be a very real issue. Perhaps the biggest hurdle of all is that high initial cost. A system that can save about 2200 to 3000 kWh a year might cost you about $3,000. Of course, this all depends on where you are and your roof's amount of solar exposure. The further south you're located, the more hours are in a solar day. Typically, it's four hours in the northern United States, increasing to six or seven hours further south.

As more manufacturers increase their capacity, price per kilowatt comes down. According to ConsumerAffairs.com, in January 2023, the cost for a solar panel system after tax credits ranged from $11,144 to $14,696. This varies from state to state.

Resiliency of Solar

When you install solar panels, you are helping your community prevent rolling brownouts. Heavy loads on the grid can lead to rolling blackouts. With solar panels, you can help your local utility prevent that. If you install wall batteries, you can also be grid independent. This is good if you're worried about being more resilient and disaster ready.

You don't have to install a huge, costly system if you're just worried about resiliency. Small systems initially intended for camping might be enough to charge your phone or turn on your TV to get information. For example, Rock Pals has a system for few hundred dollars.

Is There a Downside to Solar?

You might want to think about where you're going to dispose of them after 20 years. You might have concerns such as where the raw material comes from. Or you might realize that you'd prefer to use the roof area where you would need to install would be better used for other things. If I use my roof for solar panels, perhaps I can't have a small garden up there.

Solar meters linked into the grid are called net-zero. Whatever you generate in the day or during the summer you get back at night or in the winter. Some utility companies have ways around net zero. I was told that net-zero is a way to pay for the electrons but not the grid. For example, because I rely on them at night, they charge me more at night than I produce for them.

Above all consider your budget and that sometimes the rebates may not come in, or that they will come in later than you had planned.

More Resources

Where we live in L.A. County, we can view the L.A. County solar map at solar-map.lacounty.gov. This website allows you to look at your own roof and see the orientation and number of panels that would be required to meet your home's needs.

Depending on where you live, you may be able to get money for low carbon fuel credits, especially if you own an electric vehicle. This varies a lot by state and municipality, but some research and legwork might pay off.

Julie with her family's electric and hybrid cars.

Grid Alternatives, a California nonprofit, is helping communities nationwide to get affordable solar power and solar jobs. You can volunteer, learn installation, and get other technical assistance there.

Personal Example

In 2016, we put in our PV system, along with a new highly reflective roof, and an EV charging station. The system generates about 7KW and cost about $10,000 dollars. Where an average vehicle relies on about 480 gallons of

A portable solar panel charges the battery unit, with a built-in inverter. The light is plugged into the battery unit.

fuel to travel 12,000 miles, our Leaf offset about $2,000 in fuel costs alone. With the plug-in Prius, that was about double. The electric bill went down from $200 to about $35 per month. Moreover, there is a banked amount at Los Angeles Department of Water and Power (to whom we pay our bill) of about $800 from over-generation.

Julie in the field with a portable solar panel, battery unit, and light.

In effect, our system paid for itself in four years and is expected to generate $5,000 a year in fuel offsets. There are so many ways to become energy independent. The solar array eliminated most of the household and vehicle power costs. A penny saved is truly a penny earned.

Electric cars are amazing and wonderful to drive. Many other small devices can be solar-powered freeing one from being tied to power companies. These devices can be used for indoor/outdoor lights, camping, computers, phones, radios, fans, to name several.

Chapter 5

General Hygiene and Clothing

TOILETS

A toilet is a necessity in any household. It doesn't matter if the household is in a poor rural community, a rich household of the Roman empire, or just an average American home. We all need the toilet.

IN A NUTSHELL

- Simple flush toilet alternatives
- Personal hygiene and dry brushing
- Clothes laundering and maintenance
- Natural cleansers

For our purposes here, we might learn the most from those communities that have less developed infrastructure but have found a way to safely deal with human waste without creating a health hazard. Health authorities point out that in the aftermath of any major disaster, the deaths that result from the lack of infrastructure—such as no running water, no hot water, no functioning toilets, no medical supplies or personnel—are often greater than the deaths from the disaster itself.

Members of some "intentional communities" who want to be off the grid and practice a more ecological way to process wastes learn quickly what works and what doesn't.

Consider that in the vast sweep of human existence, outhouses were one of the main ways to deal with human waste. In rural communities of the United States, outhouses were still common during the first half of the twentieth century, before indoor plumbing sent all the wastewater to a local processing facility or septic tanks.

An outhouse is usually just a privacy structure over a pit, hopefully located so that the water table is

This type of sturdy outhouse design can be built from recycled wood and is long lasting.

not affected. Outhouses are by no means obsolete; the porta potty that you see at every construction site is just a portable outhouse.

High-tech composting toilets, such as the Clivus Multrum composting toilet, have been around for at least fifty years. But most of the composting toilets are expensive.

For those on a budget, let's consider some of the low-cost toilet alternatives. Such a toilet can be used as an outback toilet where there is no plumbing, as an alternative to the conventional flush toilet, or as the toilet to be used after an emergency when existing infrastructure is destroyed.

COMPOST TOILET

A compost toilet is simply some sort of container where waste can be disposed. The contents are collected and quickly or slowly decompose until you empty the contents into your garden or orchard. Some are large enough that the contents can be naturally decomposed; others require a low amount of electricity to work.

Prices for purpose-made composting toilets vary from about $300 to as much as $4,000, so the choice depends on your needs and your budget.

For those willing to purchase one, I suggest you simply go online and start searching. See what fits your needs.

An emergency toilet.

However, if all you need is a toilet to use in emergencies, then all you really need is a bucket and a toilet seat that snaps onto the bucket.

RV TOILET

A portable RV toilet is essentially a bucket within a bucket, with a seat and a lid. (This is different from a built-in RV toilet, which usually has a holding tank.) These toilets are sold at RV stores and sporting goods stores. They are easy to use and must be emptied regularly.

Author Christopher Nyerges in his book *How to Survive Anywhere* documented using an RV toilet in his home as a one-month experiment. The essence of the experiment was that this toilet was used exclusively for a full month, with the toilet contents emptied into a trench in the yard. After each emptying, the contents were covered with straw, earthworms, and soil. Eventually, tomatoes were grown in the trench. In the bathroom, the main challenge was combating the odor. Nyerges did not want to use the blue disinfectant given with the toilet, because the safety of the blue disinfectant was uncertain in soil. Nyerges experimented with lemons, baking soda, and wood ash. Because he used a wood stove in his household, Nyerges opted to use wood ash because it was a cheap and readily available resource. The wood ash was added to the toilet after each use, and according to the records he kept, there was no bad odor or flies in the bathroom.

That was a simple and inexpensive toilet alternative, and its use is available to anyone with the outdoor space to empty the bucket.

WHITE BUCKET

Another toilet option is to purchase a plastic toilet seat designed to snap onto any five-gallon bucket. Though perhaps not quite as comfortable as the portable RV toilet, it is nevertheless a quick and easy toilet to put together. It is also possible to use a plastic liner in the bucket to make cleaning easier. However, though it makes the bucket easier to clean, you must then decide what you're going to do with the bag. If you are merely going to dispose of the bags at a municipal dump, then perhaps this is an OK option. However, since I feel that local composting of the contents is the best long-term and most sustainable option, I suggest simply using the bucket without a plastic liner, having added sawdust to the bucket before use, and adding a bit of sawdust after each use. This helped to absorb some moisture, and the entire contents can be buried when full.

COMMODE CHAIR (HOSPITAL POTTY)

Yet another simple option for the home emergency toilet is to obtain the type of portable toilet available from medical suppliers that are sometimes given to elderly patients or others with mobility issues. These can be a bit expensive when new. But if you want one and can afford it, by all means you should purchase one.

As an alternative to buying one new, investigate thrift stores and watch for them at yard sales. You'd be surprised how often they are sold for between $5 and $20.

COMMUNITY OUTHOUSE METHODS

A friend shared the details his "intentional community," where the members (among other things) wanted to live naturally, grow their own food,

Kevin Sutherland inspects a standard hospital potty. (Photo by Christopher Nyerges.

and live in a sustainable manner. This meant that they used compost toilets. The small brick house that they built as the outhouse looked very much like the bathrooms you see at parks and campgrounds. The toilets were all set up against one wall, and their contents were deposited in a large holding tank underneath. Sawdust was poured over the fresh contents after each use.

The holding tanks were designed like large bins that could be pulled out from the rear of the building. Workers emptied these large bins when they got full into another holding area, where it was covered with more sawdust and allowed to sit for about two months. They found that there was no odor associated with this system, and that the contents became an easily usable fertilizer, mostly for fruit trees and non-food crops.

WORM FARM

The worm farm is another toilet alternative, assuming you have a private outdoor area. This was practiced by one of our associates in his own backyard. It was very simple and didn't cost him any outlay of cash because he had all the supplies already.

A commode chair was placed in a private part of his yard, with simply a wooden crate underneath (he removed the bowl). Each time he used this toilet, he shoveled on some earthworms and soil. When the crate was full, he simply left it there and moved the chair, positioning it above another crate. By the time the second one was full, he dug around with a trowel and saw that all the contents of the first crate had been fully decomposed by the action of the earthworms, so the contents were emptied on his fruit trees.

TOILET PAPER

Don't forget to store a good amount of toilet paper. Like everyone else, I was both amused and disturbed that toilet paper was one of the first things that people began to hoard as the 2020 pandemic began. Toilet paper is a good barter item in an emergency.

I have elderly relatives who could not get toilet paper during the Great

Depression, and for some, during World War II. What did they do? They used newspaper and non-glossy sheets of paper from magazines and catalogs. Most everyone had an outhouse back then, so there was no worry about the drain line getting clogged. Some explained that they also used various leaves!

TOILET CLOTH

Toilet paper is a relatively recent invention. When the 2020 pandemic put toilet paper in the spotlight, I noticed that people began to think twice about their dependence on it. Reusable toilet paper has become a trend known by various names, and it seems destined to receive more popular consideration.

Using cloth is by no means a new practice. People have been laundering cloth diapers for infants for many years, and doing this also seems to have been rediscovered as toilet cloth. According to buzzfeed.

An array of colorful toilet cloth.

com, "It's pretty simple: It's a cost effective, eco-friendly system in which you wipe with cloth wipes instead of toilet paper, and then wash and reuse them for as long as they last."

There are obvious concerns about making sure whatever you use is clean to start with and handled in a hygienic way after. This means washing in very hot water, possibly with bleach in the water, or sun drying, as sunlight sterilizes as well.

Do your research! Unsafe handling can cause serious illness, such as infections from harmful strains of *E. coli* bacteria. According to

Healthline.com, such cloths must be handled carefully, and their website gives guidelines as well as the pros and cons in their article "All About Reusable Toilet Paper: What You Should Know."

The upside to this trend is that if more people practice this it will mean harvesting fewer trees. You save money with this system, but it may use more water and possibly will take more time.

PRIVACY SCREEN

Keep in mind that if you choose to use an alternative toilet in your backyard, you may want some sort of privacy screen. You can just buy a simple portable "closet," designed to hang a solar water shower.

If you're on a really tight budget and can't afford one, you can just run a few clothes-lines around your toilet area and hang some sheets, tarps, or blankets. I've done this both in the backyard, and while camping in the desert. It's relatively easy to do.

This is a privacy closet sold in backpacking stores. It folds down to very little space when not in use.

STAYING CLEAN WITH MINIMAL WATER

I don't think I need to emphasize that it's important to keep the body clean. It's not just about odor—the skin is an organ of excretion and must be cleaned. Diseases can be hard to control if there isn't an easy way to wash the body, clean wounds, and maintain cleanliness of our surroundings.

In the United States, the availability of water is largely taken for granted. In the cities, water is piped in from wherever the closest source happens to be. In rural areas, people have piped water, but also wells and storage containers.

We should appreciate every drop of water and do our very best to not waste it.

If and when water is scarce, you could bathe outside so that the water drains into your garden and is thereby used twice—for your washing and for the garden.

BRUSH BATHS

When water is scarce and you can't spare any for a shower or bath, you should take a "brush bath." This is where you take the stiffest brush you can tolerate, and simply brush every square inch of your skin. This removes dead skin cells and gives you a remarkable feeling of freshness, even without water.

Some years ago, the members of our organization spent time in the desert learning survival skills. Though these outings were only for a few days in the desert, everyone on the trip practiced keeping their bodies clean without water. Everyone chose a brush that would be comfortable on their skin, and many chose a Fuller brush. Though it was designed for scrubbing sinks and floors, most of the attendees found that it was very suitable for skin.

Handled scrub brush preferred by many for a brush bath.

When I've used this method, I've scrubbed my entire body with the brush. Sometimes, you could actually see the dead skin cells as they came off, usually looking like a fine dust. Although some people find this uncomfortable at first, nearly everyone feels "clean" and invigorated afterwards.

HAND-WASHING CLOTHES

The earliest washing machines—the mechanical hand-crank ones that preceded the electrical ones—were designed because people got tired of washing clothes by hand. But let's not forget that people hand-washed their clothes for thousands of years. The average person has simply forgotten how to do it!

But it's really not that hard. And if the power goes out, you're still going to want to remain clean.

Add a few articles of clothing to a bucket or tub, add hot water and soap, and then just squeeze and brush away. It's good exercise, and you'll probably get cleaner clothes than you do with a modern washing machine.

Tim Snider washes clothes with a plunger and bucket. (Photo by Christopher Nyerges.)

Rinse the clothes, and then hang dry on your "solar clothes dryer."

Washing your clothes is a necessity to maintain your sense of freshness, even in the aftermath of a disaster. When you have minimal water, wash your clothes in a tub with some water and soap, and let the water drain into your garden.

SUN WASHING CLOTHES

If you have no water to spare for washing clothes, you can at least shake out your clothes each day, and hang them in the sun for a few hours. That's not the same as washing them with water, but the UV rays of the sun do help somewhat in disinfecting. Let your clothes hang in the sun for an hour or more, then turn them inside out and let them hang for another hour.

SOAPS FROM NATURE

You should have plenty of soap stored in your household, not just for emergencies, but because you need to stay clean to stay healthy. But what happens when you run out of soap? The store shelves are empty!

Throughout North America, many plants have been used for millennia for soap because of their high saponin content. There are many more soap plants than the ones described here. To learn about your area's local soap plants, talk to someone at a native plant society or in the botany department of a college or university.

Here is a short listing of some of the soap plants found in nature, and which can be easily grown in your yard.

AMOLE
(Chlorogalum pomeridianum)

There is a fairly widespread member of the lily family with a tennis-ball-size bulb referred to as amole, found chiefly in the western United States. The long linear leaves measure a foot and longer, and they are wavy on their margins. When you dig down—sometimes up to a foot deep in hard soil—you'll find the bulb, which is entirely covered in layers of brown fibers.

For soap, remove the brown fiber until you reach the white bulb. It is formed in layers, just like an onion, and you'll find it sticky and soapy to handle. Take a few layers of the white bulb, add water, and agitate between your hands. A rich lather results, which you can use to take a bath, wash your clothes, or clean your dog.

Amole.

BOUNCING BET
(Saponaria officinalis)

Bouncing Bet, also known as soapwort, is widespread. It is commonly planted as a garden plant for its pink flowers and occurs wild in some areas. It is an introduced plant with little history of use by Native Americans.

The leaves or the roots can be used, though I prefer to use the leaves simply because once you pull the root, the plant is gone. Bouncing Bet is made into soap by agitating the fresh leaves between your hands with water. The quality of lather varies, but it is worth knowing about should the plant grow abundantly in your area.

MOUNTAIN LILAC
(Ceanothus species)

Mountain lilac is a shrub to a small tree, fairly common throughout the western United States, with various species found throughout the United States. There are many species that can be used for soap. Since the botanical features of each species varies, the easiest way to determine if

Mountain Lilac.

you have a mountain lilac is to take a handful of blossoms, add water, and rub between your hands. You'll get a good lather with a mild aroma if you have mountain lilac.

By late spring to early summer, the flowers fall off and tiny, sticky, green fruits develop. These too can be rubbed between the hands with water to make a good soap. The fruits can also be dried and then reconstituted later when soap is needed. The mountain lilac also makes a very attractive landscaping plant.

YUCCA
(Hesperoyucca whipplei)

There are numerous species of yucca found widely, mostly throughout the Plains and Western states. They resemble big pin cushions, with long, linear, needle-tipped leaves. Though the use of the root for soap has been widely popularized, I have found that one need only cut one leaf to make soap. When you cut off the leaf, be very careful not to poke yourself with one of the sharp tips nor slice your fingers on the very sharp edges. Strip the leaf into fibers until you have a handful of very thin strands. Then, add water, agitate between your hands, and you have a good quality soap.

Angelo Cervera examines a yucca plant. Yucca leaves, when shredded and agitated with water, produce a superior soap.

SEWING AND MENDING

Growing up in the 1960s and 1970s, there was still a focus on practical self-sufficiency as a part of the basics of education. Skills such as those taught in "home economics" classes included techniques of sewing and food preparation. The schools and most parents at that time recognized the importance of these basic skills.

In recent times, very few people have continued to make sewing a part of their lives. A combination of "throw-away culture," and the mass

A simple portable sewing kit.

production of products requiring sewing, shifted production of basic items to countries where they could be made cheaply and where workers receive much lower pay. That shift has resulted in the art of sewing nearly disappearing in this country.

Sewing seems to have been given a bad connotation, especially with images coming to mind of women performing tasks considered "unnecessary" in modern times. There is also that image of Suzie Homemaker being out of touch, as a gender-polarized pigeonholed image for women and girls. And yet, despite all that, sewing is an essential skill!

Historically, both men and women constructed remarkable, exceptionally useful items by sewing and handwork. Much fine art, such as tapestries and embroidery, have embellished our lives. Countless useful items have been crafted to make life better and more beautiful.

Some of the benefits of sewing I've experienced are much like the benefits of art. There is a creative element at play. You choose the materials, colors, design, and construction techniques (stitches, finishing techniques, buttons, fasteners, etc.). The possibilities are endless.

Our next-door neighbor, Mrs. Savluk, taught me how to sew a few simple items after school when I was growing up. I learned some embroidery skills at Girl Scouts during elementary school and made a few items

Foot-powered sewing machine. (Photo courtesy of Lehman's.)

in middle-school home economics classes. Then, in college, I got interested in making clothing as a business, so I took a couple of classes at the nearby community college. I made my own shirts, dresses, skirts, and pants, and I learned how to sew on buttons and zippers. For me, it was an incredible awakening to the art of construction, putting together pieces of fabric and all that goes with it to complete a project.

My brain was making new connections and I was gaining new competencies and skills. Scientifically speaking, I was using new brain areas. The feeling of wearing something I had created was

Julie with an apron she made and decorated.

unique and an incredible experience for someone raised almost solely on new store-bought clothing. Looking at what I had made was inspiring to me.

As a young mother, I made aprons out of a strong canvas fabric which I then hand-painted. This was a way for me to earn some extra income and was a learning opportunity.

As a child, I was aware of my grandmother's skills as a seamstress. During the Great Depression, she designed and sewed stylish clothes for my mother to prepare for her university stay. The clothes made such an impact that her college mates thought she was an aristocrat. My grandmother made her own linen tablecloths, curtains, aprons, and sometimes clothes for us grandchildren. It seemed that she did this almost automatically and quite easily, like riding a bike.

For her, sewing was not just a survival skill—it was also a way of expressing her love, care, and concern for all of us.

What do you need in a basic sewing kit?

1. A good pair of sharp scissors.
2. Needles of varying sizes for different tasks.
3. Thread of varying types—make sure to have an adequate supply.
4. A sturdy and waterproof container to keep these in.

SEWING AS A SURVIVAL SKILL

Maybe you need a tent because your home is now destroyed or unsafe, and it's windy or raining. Or an essential clothing item has a large rip, or is missing, due to the conditions of the emergency. You need to make something essential from whatever materials are available. For instance, a simple poncho can be fashioned from a wool blanket.

MAKING A PONCHO

Making a poncho from a blanket is about a simple as you can get. Do you remember Clint Eastwood in *The Good, the Bad, and the Ugly*, traveling during the Civil War looking for treasure? In one scene, he covered a dying soldier with his coat and then took a blanket from the soldier, which became his character's iconic poncho.

The blanket poncho is simple to make and has been in use for at least centuries in Mexico and South America.

Yes, the blanket poncho is simply a blanket with a slit cut into the middle . . . anyone can do that! But let's

Angelo Cervera shows a Mexican blanket-style poncho. He sometimes wears it with a belt, as shown here.

look at a few of the details that make this a garment that you'll enjoy wearing and enjoy being seen wearing. Remember, this will be one of your easiest sewing projects ever.

The selection of the blanket is first. Choose a fabric that will be appropriate to when and where you will be wearing it. In colder climates, you'll want a heavier blanket, perhaps made of wool. If you're in a warmer climate, you might select a cotton blanket.

I suggest that you do as I did for my first poncho. Go to a flea market or thrift store and spend as little as possible to buy a used blanket. After you get the hang of it, you might use better blankets.

Now, take a look at your blanket. Most blankets are rectangular, not square. When you wear the blanket as a poncho, you want the long side to come up the front of your body and down the back, which leaves the sides open for your arms. It's possible that in certain cases, you may want the poncho to be worn side-to-side, but that is not the norm.

Then, cut a slit about a foot-and-a-half-long in the middle of the blanket. The slit should be parallel to the long side of the blanket, which gives your neck room to move forward and backward. I suggest that you cut the slit just big enough to fit over your head at first, and then make it bigger as needed. When you are comfortable with the length of the slit, you should hem the edge. That simply means that you wrap the cut edge with thread so that the loose threads of the opening do not continually unravel. You could also get some hem material or another fabric and cover your slit with that—all depends on how you want to customize the look of your new blanket-poncho.

One of the things that I always do with a new sewing project is to start a pattern using paper, rather than the fabric. So, if you have never done a sewing project, you may first want to practice on a large sheet of paper, as large as the blanket you'll be working with. (Since most people don't have paper that large, simply tape sheets of newspaper or paper bags together until you get the desired size.) Then cut your slit and put on the paper poncho to get a sense of how it fits (or doesn't fit). By working with a paper model, you can tweak your pattern. Then when you finally work with your chosen material, you're guaranteed success. Though this is an extra step, I think it actually saves you time and money in the long run.

Anyway, that's all there is to it! You've sewn your first poncho!

FIRST AID

We spoke with Art Lee, a man with an engineering background from Southern California, who showed WTI active members how he puts together his own first aid kits by purchasing all the components individually—even buying many of the items from the 99-cent store! He has two DIY kits, one for backpacking and one for home use.

"I made my own because I felt I could get it all cheaper with precisely what I want," said Lee. "Too many of the pre-packaged kits are overpriced and just contain a lot of band-aids. I wanted something that is economical, compact, and geared to my personal needs."

Lee emphasizes that one should always pick and choose for their own needs. For example, a diabetic will have certain needs, and a parent with children will have other specific needs. Though I use no pharmaceuticals, I leave them on the list to indicate the types of ailments you may want to address with medicines in your kit.

LEVEL ONE: PORTABLE FIRST AID KIT

"I can get 80 percent of these ingredients by going to two or three 99-cent stores, and maybe Walmart," said Lee. He shops around for the lowest prices; some items are purchased online.

PORTABLE FIRST AID KIT CONTENTS

- Two (4-inch-square) gauze pads
- Two (4-inch-square) non-stick pads
- One large Israeli trauma pad
- Two 25-gram size QuikClot® or Celox™
- Four nitrile gloves
- Four alcohol pads
- One pair splinter tweezers
- One roll (one-inch) adhesive tape
- One moleskin
- One container of tincture of iodine
- Six (½-inch) Band-Aids.

Art Lee shows a selection of basic first aid supplies.

Art Lee's medical supplies all fit into a small bag. For trail use, compactness and portability are essential.

- Six (¾-inch) Band-Aids
- Two (2-inch) Band-Aids
- Two (¼-inch) Steri-strips
- Two (½-inch) Steri-strips
- Four butterfly closures
- One container of instant glue
- Three maxi-pads (to absorb bleeding)
- One container Visine®
- One nail clipper
- One small flashlight
- One hand-sanitizer container
- Five Q-tips®
- One tube ChapStick®
- One tube of antibiotic ointment
- 16 (200-mg) doses ibuprofen
- 8 (2 mg) doses Loperamide/Lomotil (for diarrhea)
- 8 doses antihistamine (for allergies)
- 8 multi-vitamins

All of this fits into Lee's little zippered pouch and is easily carried on the trail. Fortunately, he's only had to use the items in his kit for a few minor incidents on the trail (and that's how we like it, right?).

LEVEL TWO: HOME FIRST AID KIT

Obviously, there's more in this kit and it's bigger and heavier. It's for all those home emergencies, when you don't want to hunt around the house for what you need.

HOME FIRST AID KIT CONTENTS

- CPR mask
- Gloves
- Wet wipes
- Hand sanitizer

INSTRUMENTS

- A flashlight
- Scissors
- Splinter tweezers
- Sharp tweezers
- Large nail clipper
- Large safety pins
- Single edge razor
- Knife

FOR WOUNDS

- One (20-cc) irrigating syringe
- Assorted sizes of bandages (Band-Aids)
- Steri-strip
- Butterfly tape
- Duct tape (yes, duct tape really comes in handy for many things)
- Adhesive tape

- Tegaderm™ (this is a non-adhesive film by 3M, a breathable band-aid, one of the more expensive components of the kit)
- Moleskin
- 4-inch-square gauze pads
- 2-inch-square gauze
- QuikClot® gauze
- Non-stick gauze pads
- Roll of gauze
- Israeli trauma pad
- Q-tips®
- Nylon suture
- Cyanoacrylate glue (yes, folks, "superglue")
- 1 (three-inch) ACE™ wrap
- Triangular bandage
- Roller dressing

PILLS AND OTHER SUPPLIES

- Tylenol®
- Ibuprofen
- Aspirin
- Claritin®
- 1% hydrocortisone cream
- anti-diarrhea pills
- fever thermometer
- alcohol pads
- cold pack
- lip balm
- triple antibiotic ointment
- Salonpas® pain relief patch
- A pen

If purchased economically, the contents of Lee's level-one pack can be obtained for about $30 to $40, and Lee's level-two pack for between $100 and $150.

He reminds people to not slavishly follow someone else's list, but to customize according to your needs. And remember, all the first aid gear in the world is of limited value if you haven't learned how to actually use them in an emergency. To that end, Lee has taken various Red Cross first aid courses, and encourages readers to do likewise.

Note: If you prefer "natural" remedies, I recommend that you take the time to study applied herbal wisdom. Many people looking for alternatives refer to *Healing with Medicinal Plants of the West* by Dr. James Adams and books by herbalist Michael Moore.

Chapter 6
Resources

Hard times come and go, and as an insightful person once said, "No storm stays forever." True, and yet it's still a good long-term idea to live frugally and learn how to make things. In so much survival literature, the focus is on guns, knives, survival kits, food storage, solar power, and all manner of off-the-grid and self-reliant skills and gear. But how much investment is truly necessary?

First, please note that everything in this book is about finding ways to live better on less. That means, among other things, getting more mileage out of each dollar. It also means that you should seriously think before every purchase. Differentiate between needs and wants. Do I really need that expensive sweater? Or could I buy 15 items of excellent quality at Goodwill at the same cost?

If you're an average person reading this book, a lot of the "stuff" that you currently have, you'll never need—it will only clutter up your life and deflate your wallet. I learned this the hard way, and—unfortunately—lots of people seem destined to learn it the hard way too. Oh, well! Just remember that a deal and discount isn't always a deal. Another perspective is that you're often richer not because of all the stuff you possess, but because of the degree that you can do *without* all that stuff. Your own inner abilities and qualities of character are the riches that you actually have. This doesn't mean to conclude it is best to be poor. Money and things have their value, but it is a problem when we serve and are enslaved by stuff. If you arrange your life so that it serves your inner development, it hardly matters if you live in an attic or a tent or in a mansion.

RESOURCES AND RECYCLING

You know, most folks in the United States are blind to the fact that we have so many resources at our disposal. We are so blind to how fortunate we are that we constantly and continually throw good things into the trash, blindly focused on "something new," with little concern about our excessive use of resources.

I am deeply concerned about this for at least two reasons.

One, as a student of the Law of Thought, I see that if I waste, or anyone wastes, we will be without. If I do not use the resources that come into my hands wisely, I will earn not having those resources. This, in part, explains what Jesus meant when he said the poor will be with us always. Poverty is primarily a state of mind, which, if persisted over long periods of time, results in lack. It is our resistance to learning that keeps us in this state.

And secondly, if we do not learn to see that resources are abundant, our suffering will be all the greater if and when there are crises (tornado, earthquake, trucker strikes, famine, etc.) which limit our resources. If we make the effort to get much better use of the material resources we have, we will weather the storm and usually be stronger from the experience.

Over the years at our organization's educational programs, various officers and members tried to specialize in showing people that they can often recycle and reuse many of the resources that they routinely discard. Among the many benefits of doing this is your growing ability to see endless possibilities. This is a valuable ability.

Talal shows son Gabriel how to fix a lamp, rather than unceremoniously throwing it into the trash.

A penny saved is a penny earned. You can repair things and not need to buy them. Repairing and refurbishing are ways to save your money and also many of the skills built to do this may be monetizable.

One way to learn about repairing things and get to know your community at the same time is to visit a "repair café," with over 2,500 locations around the world and over 100 in the United States. You can visit www.repaircafe.org to find out how to repair many household and everyday items using their repair guides, and to meet with volunteers who offer services to the community and teach many valued skills. They can help you start your own repair café in your area or to volunteer.

CLOTHING AND FABRICS

Clothes that can still be worn by someone ought not be tossed into a trash can. Usable garments that you no longer wear, or that you've outgrown, should be taken to one of the many organizations that provide clothing to those in need. Proper care for one's clothes and garments will likewise extend their useful life.

Recently I went to a large commercial fabric store to purchase wool felt to embroider-stitch over the moth holes in cashmere sweaters. They carried an interesting "how to" book on valuing your clothes enough to mend them. Paging through it, I noticed that one of the book's pages had been torn and was taped back together. I asked the clerk if she could lower the cost. She suggested $10 but ended up giving it to me for free as it was nonexistent in her computerized inventory! According to her records, it hadn't been carried in the store since January 1971! She also recommended the website Pinterest for excellent "how to" examples of specific crochet techniques to enhance and save holey wool sweaters.

In this case, one door closed: my sweaters had become unwearable! Then, when seeking the solution, three doors opened:

1. The needed book miraculously appeared—for free! (This unique book *Mending Life: A Handbook for Repairing Clothes and Hearts*, is a classic that captures the enriching value and practice of mending. As one book reviewer put it: "There is a lesson here in cherishing rather than discarding our belongings, which may begin to change US along the way as well.")
2. The kind salesperson gave more solutions for repairing sweaters to discover on Pinterest.
3. I can now share both 1 & 2 with you!

COTTON SHEETS

Cotton sheets that are no longer in shape to use on a bed can still be pressed into service. Cut into squares and hemmed, these make ideal bandanas or kerchiefs. And kerchiefs—either for the hiker or city dweller—have MANY uses.

Clean cotton sheets can be cut into squares, short strips, and long strips. Fold them neatly and add them to your first aid kit.

A piece of cotton can be cut and sewn into a cone shape and used as a reusable coffee filter.

For those who know how to weave, old sheets and bedspreads can be made into serviceable wash cloths, throw rugs, and dog beds.

SOCKS

The number of people who darn their socks seems to dwindle every year. Are there many of you out there anymore? For large holes in socks, small sections of other fabric can be sewn over the hole to significantly extend the life of the sock.

If you have a large family and find that you wear out a lot of socks, you might consider saving those holey socks and making a blanket. Generally, you'll need about a hundred socks for a blanket.

Prudence shows the socks that she mended by hand.

The toe end of a sock can be neatly cut off and the sock can be worn as a elbow warmer. This will work the best with knee socks, but you can try it with socks of any size.

CARPETS

Insoles for shoes and boots help to keep the feet warm and provide a snugger fit for shoes that are slightly too big. An excellent insole can be made by cutting a piece from an old carpet.

Sections or rolls of old carpeting work amazingly well as a mulch, even in areas where you want to control wild grasses or other persistent weeds. You can first scythe down the existing weeds or grasses, although this isn't always necessary. Strips of carpets along outdoor walkways help to hold in moisture and contribute to improving the soil by preventing erosion and retaining moisture.

CARPET PADDING

Old-fashioned fibrous carpet padding is an ideal material to put into the bottom of pots before planting. This is the carpet padding that has the appearance of hemp or horsehair, not the modern padding which appears to be manufactured from some sort of spongy plastic. Carpet padding in pots retains moisture and provides an excellent home for earthworms.

Old carpets are laid on this steep unpaved driveway to reduce erosion from rain.

SHOES

When Michael Rubalcava was ten years old, he had a small nursery of "survival plants" at the WTI nonprofit headquarters in Los Angeles. He used cans, plastic containers, and recycled pots. He also used old shoes. He saved his outgrown shoes, filled them with soil, and grew plants in them. While participants there often laughed about them, they always sold well.

BLANKETS AND DRAPES

There are countless uses for old blankets and drapes, such as seat covers for cars, carpets, donations to charity, etc. The rag bag should be the last resort.

Author Christopher Nyerges shared that a friend of his, Christine Zellich, used to wear a pack during her local mountain hikes that she made from old drapes. Christine said that she first designed a simple pack out of paper, and folded the paper to make sure the pieces would fit. The bulk of the pack was one folded piece of the drape, with two rectangular side panels, and carrying straps. Due to the strength of the original curtains, it was a sturdy day pack.

GLASS BOTTLES AND JARS

Whether clear, brown, green, or other color, these glass bottles and jars can all be easily recycled. The simplest way is to rinse them after use, and then give them to your curbside recycler or take them to the local recycling center. But here are some other practical uses of those commonly discarded glass containers.

CANDLE MOLDS

Virtually any shape of bottle or jar can be used as a candle mold.

Candle making is relatively simple. First insert your wick into the container, securing it so that it stays in the center. Pour your wax a little at a time, preferably in one-inch increments. Let it set and harden somewhat. Do the second pouring shortly after the first has hardened a little, and then continue this way until the mold is full. Don't remove the mold until the wax is thoroughly hardened.

STORAGE

Glass jars are excellent in the garage or workshop for storing all those nails and tacks and screws and drill bits and nuts and bolts and staples and hinges and other little items that need to be organized and visible. We suggest that you save jars of the same size so that they'll all fit neatly onto your garage shelves.

Glass jars are also ideal for most kitchen storage. Grains, cereals, and pasta are best taken out of their paper or cloth containers—which renders them susceptible to roaches, rats, and spoilage—and stored in glass containers.

SOLAR TEA

It is a bit humorous that someone is making money selling "glass solar tea makers." I have always just rinsed my old gallon jars out, added water and tea leaves, and set them in the sun. I wouldn't consider paying for a jar with a plastic spigot. Any glass jar can be used for making solar tea!

METALS

Most metals can be recycled, and we should find a way for metals to be reused rather than simply discarding the item in a trash can. Some recycling centers will accept "tin" cans, all will accept aluminum, and many will accept brass and copper metals.

Often, old appliances are full of recyclable metals and shouldn't just be tossed away. In fact, you'd be surprised to discover how much useable material you'd find on the average tossed-out TV, refrigerator, water heater, dish washer, etc.

IRON WATER

One way to repurpose metals is to create "iron water" for fertilizing potted plants and trees. Fill a five-gallon plastic bucket with crushed cans, old nails, other metal items, and water, and cover it. Within a few weeks, the cans rust, and the water turns brown. It's surprising how quickly the rusting process occurs. I've seen the entire contents of two buckets rust away to nothing in about seven months. This brown, rusty water is a good source of iron for your plants.

Use it sparingly, often diluting it with fresh water. This works out especially well if the soil in our area has a low iron content.

Julie pours the water from the iron-water bucket onto nearby plants.

WATERING CAN

A simple watering can is easy to make with a large fruit juice can. Punch many holes in the bottom of the can with a nail, then attach a handle to the top of the can (you can use an old wire clothes hanger).

PLANTERS

Virtually any used can is a potential planter. This includes every can size, from small cat-food and tuna cans for small succulents and cacti, to soup cans, to large cans used for restaurants and cafeteria food. They can all be made into planters.

TOOL HOLDER

It's easy to forget hand tools in your garden. One way to get the tools off the ground and in a safe place is to mount a large coffee can on the back side of a fence or gate, or perhaps on a garden post.

Drill a hole into the can towards the top, and then screw the can into the fence or gate with a wood screw. (If you think that rainwater might collect in the can, drill a few holes into the bottom of the can.) Any of these items can be painted with leftover paint for even longer usefulness. This could be a good children's project!

A CAMPER'S CAN-DO

Campers and hikers fabricate many items from old cans. A large can serves well as a stove. With the lid cut off, you can simply invert the can, punch a few holes, and cook on the "top" of the can. Your fire will be inside the can, and you can even cut a little "door" to facilitate the introduction of more twigs.

A large can may also be used as a pot. Just add your soup or stew and simmer over the fire. A smaller can is used as a cup or bowl.

Note: Make sure that any can you repurpose was not made with lead solder; most modern cans do not contain lead. Also, some cans have a plastic liner. If you're going to use your can for cooking, you should burn out that liner first by putting the can into a fire, upside down, and letting the liner burn away.

HOBO LANTERN

Friends of mine have made many hobo lanterns over the years and find them remarkably useful. There's nothing complicated here.

Though we've seen many ways to make a lantern out of an old aluminum can, here is the method we prefer these days, largely because it is the easiest, and it works well.

A hobo lantern, made by putting a candle into a used aluminum can.

With the can upright, cut a vertical slit from top to bottom, and then make a horizontal slip at the top and bottom of the vertical slit (The cut will look like a sideways H). Now you have two "doors." Hang the lantern by the flip-top, and simply insert a candle into the can. You might need to melt the bottom of the candle to keep it secure. The "doors" often help to turn the lantern away from the wind.

HANGING PLANTER

An old metal bucket that's full of holes needn't be tossed in the trash. We've seen buckets in poor condition that were simply filled with soil, a vining plant planted, and then hung on a hook or from a tree limb. These can be quite attractive and "shabby-chic."

BIRD FEEDERS

The easiest bird feeder is made by hanging an old hub cap or pie pan from three wires. The hub cap can then be filled with water or birdseed.

Another easy-to-make bird feeder is one half of a coconut shell. Again, simply secure three wires or cords and hang it up. (If you try to make holes in the coconut with a nail, you might crack it. To be safe, drill the holes.)

WINDOW SCREEN

If you're a gardener, you'll always have a use for old window screen. Whenever we plant a tree where we suspect there are gophers and moles, we first line the hole with a piece of old window screen. This protects the young roots from being chewed to death by underground feeders. The screen will slowly rust away by the time the tree is large enough to not be affected by gophers and moles, and that rusting will add iron to the soil.

WIRE CLOTHES HANGERS

Wire clothes hangers can be lifesavers if you have them when you need them. Who hasn't used one to unlock a car when the keys were locked inside? Hangers can also be fabricated into plant hangers, used for makeshift repairs, used for emergency bicycle toe clips (and other emergency bicycle repairs), for repairing or replacing bucket handles, for holding up a bad exhaust pipe or muffler, as a short-term car radio antenna, and for countless other uses.

55-GALLON STORAGE DRUMS

During World War II, servicemen in the South Pacific creatively used the plentiful 55-gallon (and smaller) storage drums for all manner of applications. Many tied together were used as rafts. They used them for target practice, for outhouses, for tables, chairs, musical drums, heaters, stoves, pulleys, wheels, floats, etc. These drums are still common, and they have several useful home applications.

A quality woodstove is expensive. However, you can purchase cast-iron hardware to convert a 55- or 35-gallon drum into a woodstove.

55-gallon drums can also be made into a woodstove in the standing upright position, using only one drum. A door is cut in the lower section of the drum, approximately 10 inches square. (To do this generally requires the use of a cutting torch.) One of our members has seen 55-gallon drum woodstoves in homes in Mexico, in blacksmith shops, and in Navajo hogans of the Southwest.

SOLAR WATER HEATER

Here's an idea for heating water in the "outback" that's inexpensive and effective. Take a large one gallon can, spray the outside black (optional), and place it in direct sunlight. Cover the can with a sheet of clear plastic and secure the edges of the plastic with rocks or soil. Depending on air temperature and time of year, you'll have hot water in anywhere from a half-hour to several hours.

WATER HEATERS

Water heaters, both gas and electric, are commonly tossed out when they no longer work. But more often than not, the tanks still hold water. A cleaned-out water heater tank with no leaks can be set in a corner of your garage and filled with water. This is perhaps the easiest, most convenient, and cheapest of ways to store larger amounts of water in the event of an earthquake.

If properly plumbed and safely situated, you can use an old water heater tank as a wood-burning water heater. The tank must be set on brick or cement—perhaps a steel base would be best. The fire is built right in the bottom of the tank—in the space where the gas heating element is normally situated. The hollow space in the middle of a gas heater is a flue and also serves to help heat the water. For the water inlet, you must use a metal galvanized pipe. (A garden hose just won't do, because the water in the tank gets too hot.) There are several ways to install your outlet valve.

If you have some experience with plumbing, this explanation should be sufficient. Otherwise, talk to a plumber before you try this.

PLASTICS

Only since the late 1980s have serious efforts been made to recycle discarded plastic products. Barring unforeseeable events, they are here to stay. As of this writing, more and more plastic products are accepted by recyclers. A few manufacturers fabricate new items such as flowerpots from discarded plastic. These are steps in the right direction. But finding a way to reuse plastic products is another good option.

LARGE TRASH BAGS

What are some of the ways in which we can make use of plastic products that would otherwise be discarded?

Let's start with large plastic trash bags. If clean, these make excellent emergency raincoats. Simply cut two holes for the arms and a hole for the head. If you want a "hood," you cut the two arm holes and a hole for your face. A folded plastic bag fits easily in the glove compartment, briefcase, or daypack and is quite versatile if the need arises.

Used plastic trash bags make excellent scarecrows. Set a six-foot post in your garden—the post needn't be any thicker than a broomstick. Place the plastic bag over it and tie it off towards the top. Even with a light breeze, the plastic will flutter in the wind and make noise. The noise and constant movement of the loose parts of the plastic tends to frighten birds that might otherwise linger.

SANDWICH BAGS

The heavy-duty bags should be washed, hung out to dry, and reused. There's no reason to use these just once and then toss them.

Some of the lighter-grade ones have a shorter lifespan. One way to press these into service when they're no longer food-ready is to wear them as a "glove" while painting. Simply place the bag loosely over the hand (assuming the bag is large enough), and then secure the bag around your wrist with tape, a rubber band (not too tight!), or a piece of string.

These "plastic gloves" also come in handy for gun-cleaning or working with solvents.

JUGS

Many products are packaged in one-gallon plastic jugs, from juice and milk to bleach and liquid laundry detergent. These containers are very useful for the method of water recycling described in the chapter on water. Briefly, you can save your bath and shower water in these gallon jugs. Then, you take that water outside and water your plants, or, by pouring two gallons simultaneously into the toilet bowl, you can flush your toilet using water you've already used and paid for.

By creatively cutting a plastic jug, you can create funnels and scoops. A funnel is made by cutting off the top half and inverting it. A scoop is made by cutting off the handle of the jug along with a scoop-shaped section of the jug.

MARGARINE TUBS

Plastic margarine tubs with their tight-fitting lids are excellent storage containers. After I extract honey from my beehives, I melt down the wax and pour it into these tubs.

These tubs are good for leftovers, storing grains and seeds, and for carrying pet food while on trips. I've mounted one of these on the inside of a kitchen cabinet door for the purpose of storing scouring pads. This keeps the scouring pads conveniently located and yet out of the way.

STRAWBERRY BASKETS

Birds will often pick at newly planted plants, or newly sprouted seedlings. Undoubtedly, these are filet mignon for birds. Small plastic strawberry baskets can protect seedlings from birds quite well. Just invert one basket over each sprout and use a small pebble to hold the basket in place. Light, air, and moisture can still easily get to your seedlings, but the birds can't.

PAPER

Recycle paper! One ton of recycled paper saves seventeen trees.

STATIONERY

We inspect all the incoming mail for usable typing or stationery paper. Anything that is entirely (or mostly) clean on one side is saved in a special

Recycled paper pads still have a lot of use left.

file. My cup truly runneth over, a testament to the incredible volume of usable paper coming into every household.

FOOD PACKAGING

Food packaging, especially those with ziplock closures, can be reused as containers.

FROZEN JUICE CONTAINERS

Cylindrical containers from frozen fruit juice concentrate come in handy for candlemakers. The containers are ideal for candle molds since they're generally made of thick cardboard and a metal base.

Begin by pouring a little wax into the container, and then inserting your wick. Attach two strings over the opening of the juice container in an X. Gently secure your wick to the middle of this X so that the wick remains in the middle of the candle. To make the best candles, it's better to pour in about one inch of wax at a time, and let it begin to harden before pouring more. The whole process should take about thirty minutes.

The cardboard roll from toilet paper is used as a mold for poured-wax candles.

EMPTY PAPER TOWEL AND TOILET PAPER ROLLS

These cardboard rolls have several useful functions. They are ideal for candle molds. You can also use them to store the excess sections of long cords. Simply slip the roll over a rolled-up section of the cord. They can also be used as mailing tubes or seed containers.

These rolls can also be turned into creative napkin rings. Cut the rolls into smaller sections and then cover with aluminum foil, wrapping paper, paint, or just use them as they are.

OTHER PAPERS

Some cereal boxes are lined with heavy-duty wax paper. When the box is empty, carefully remove the wax paper, shake it out, and then flatten and store it for later use. When you need wax paper—perhaps as part of a cooking project—just pull out your handy cereal box paper.

These can also be used as bags (if sufficiently clean) or to slip over a book or other item as a dust cover.

BROWN PAPER BAGS

Who doesn't have at least a dozen good uses for brown paper bags?

Textbooks can be covered with brown paper bags—a practice probably as old as paper bags. I've seen used brown paper bags as coffee filters, rather than buying purpose-made disposable paper filters for each pot of coffee.

I've used brown paper bags as vacuum cleaner bags, and they've worked fine, all manufacturers' warnings to the contrary. As for the contents of a full vacuum cleaner bag, this is ideal material to add to your compost pit, worm farm, or as a top layer of mulch for your potted plants.

You can also create rustic colorful wrapping paper from paper bags—a great project to do with kids. Let them draw or paint their own designs, or use potatoes to create a print. (Cut the potato in half and use a paring knife to carve a design. Then paint the potato with watercolor paint and stamp the paper bags or other reused paper with the designs.)

NEWSPAPERS

Whereas everyone has at least a dozen good uses for brown paper bags, everyone has at least a hundred good uses for newspaper, from no-cost packaging material to cleaning windows.

If you have no other uses for your newspapers, do not just toss them into a trash can. Newsprint is one of the easiest materials to recycle.

Newspapers also make an excellent under-mulch in gardens. Simply lay out the papers in those areas you want to mulch, and then cover with wood chips, grass clippings, leaves, pine needles, etc. Newspapers decompose rather quickly if wet.

Shredded newspapers make a good mulch, and they can also be added to the compost pit or worm farm.

OLD BOOKS

Why, oh why, do people toss books into the trash cans? We have so many of them that we've totally lost any historical perspective on the tremendous value of books.

If you no longer need them, give them away! Sell them at a yard sale. Call a school or library and ask about donating them. Send them to a prison library. Or give them away in front of your home in your own free book library. But, please, don't throw books in your trash cans.

If you've decided that you really have no more use for it, and that its use would be rather limited to other people as well, then here's a possible project with an old book.

Take a sharp razor blade, and carefully cut out a cavity. Here you can hide coins, money, jewelry, etc. Put the book back on your bookshelf and forget about it. Hopefully, it will be a book of such little interest that no one will consider picking out that book to read.

ORGANIC MATTER

If you own a shredder, such as the top-of-the-line Kemp garden shredder, you can chip and shred all of your tree and hedge clippings, all your leaves, and—believe it or not—all of your newspapers.

Julie puts dust and other debris into the compost pile.

Dog fur and lint from the dryer (just from drying cotton, not synthetics) make excellent contributions to your compost pile and or "worm farm," as does sawdust from wood working projects.

KITCHEN SCRAPS

Before you toss away kitchen scraps into your compost pit or worm farm, let's explore some of the "higher" ways you can use these items.

PET FOOD

Leftovers and many vegetable scraps can be fed to your pets. Vegetables can be gently stewed and added to dog food. This will enable you to cut down on kibble. Francis, our husky-malamute, often looks for greens, such as fig leaves, sunflower leaves, and broccoli. Some dog food is lacking in the dark greens and other vegetable nutrients that dogs need to eat a balanced diet. You can supplement dog foods with green scraps from the kitchen waste.

If you are not already familiar with all the food dos and don'ts for your pet, be sure to find out before giving them leftovers—you may be rather surprised by which foods are toxic. Some foods can cause cats and dogs serious illness and even death. Next, have your pet taste test your free scraps—the almost compost—and maybe as with Francis, the tough broccoli stems will be a needed and treasured treat! Our cat likes the broccoli tops—cooked. Offer vegetable scraps to the other fauna as well, such as rabbits or chickens.

Francis eyes a broccoli stem "bone."

GROW IT!

You'd be surprised how many kitchen scraps that are thoughtlessly tossed away can be planted.

For example, the top inch of a carrot can be cut off, placed in water, and sprouted. After a few weeks, if you haven't allowed the carrot to dry out, you can plant the carrot top in soil. The greens can then be pinched off and added to salads, or steamed, or simply kept indoors as a ferny houseplant.

Garlic cloves that have begun to sprout should not be discarded. Place these garlic cloves in a pot and let them grow. An individual clove will produce leaves continuously, which you can carefully pick off and use as chives. Each clove multiples into an entire bulb at the end of the growing season. You can dig up the entire bulb for use, or let it continue to grow and provide you with the fresh leaves. Sprouted onions can be treated likewise.

A sprouted potato, sweet potato, or yam need not be tossed away. You can plant the entire tuber into your garden and cultivate the vines until the bulbs are mature.

Avocado seeds can be planted and turned into trees.

And so many more!

Julie holds one of her "plant children," a pineapple top, almost full grown and ready to produce more delicious pineapples!

SAVING SEEDS

Many, if not most, seeds that are commonly discarded can be saved and grown.

Most citrus seeds will readily sprout if planted while still fresh. There's no reason to dry seeds except if you wish to store them for a season or longer. I've seen the best results with citrus seeds by planting the seeds directly into the pots when the seeds were fresh. I have raised countless lemons and grapefruits this way.

COCONUT SHELLS

If fresh coconuts are carefully halved, you can then use the two shells after you've scooped out the coconut meat. The shell halves are good as rustic nut or candy bowls or for storing jewelry or coins. They can also be hung from strings and used as a bird feeder.

EGGSHELLS

Eggshells are 92% calcium carbonate, also known as lime. Save your eggshells in a pan reserved exclusively for eggshells. Keep the pan in your oven, and the pilot light temperature will slowly dry out the shells. Once the pan is full, you're ready to use these valuable shells.

Prepare the dried shells by crushing them with your fingertips. This serves to strengthen your fingers as you reduce the size and surface space while crushing the shells. The pulverizing enables the minerals to assimilate into the soil right away. Yes, you can place them in a blender or use a rolling pin, but if you use your fingertips, then both you and the plants benefit. You can do this rote activity while being on the phone or watching a television show. Interestingly, plentiful research has shown that finger exercise can activate the function of cerebral cortex in multiple brain regions and delay the decline of cognitive function.

Sprinkle the eggshell powder in your lawn (this is the same as "liming" your lawn in the spring) or lightly around the bases of those plants in need of calcium. I generally fertilize our roses, calcium-hungry collard greens, and fruit trees with our powdered eggshell. Yet another benefit of eggshells is that they tend to act as a snail repellant.

COFFEE GROUNDS

Don't toss away your coffee grounds! Save these in a pan in your oven. When your pan is full, sprinkle the grounds around the base of all your acid-loving plants. All will benefit from the occasional mulch.

Used coffee grounds contain about 2 percent nitrogen, about a third of a percent of phosphoric acid, and varying amounts of potash, generally less than one percent. Coffee ground analysis shows that it contains many minerals, carbohydrates, sugars, some vitamins, and, of course, caffeine. Used grounds are particu-

Racina spreading coffee grounds around a rose.

larly good for plants such as avocados, camellias, roses, azaleas, certain evergreens, blueberries, and certain fruit trees.

DRIED CITRUS PEELS

Citrus peels decompose quickly in the compost pit. However, if you have a citrus tree, here's a way to provide it with the specific "food" that makes it healthy. Save your citrus peels (and let the peels dry in the oven or sun. When dry, break them into smaller pieces by hand. Sprinkle the citrus peel powder in thin layers around the base of your tree.

COMPOSTING METHODS

Every kitchen should have a container for collecting peelings and stems and all those parts of fruits and vegetables that you don't eat. A garbage disposal is an example of mechanization run wild. We don't need garbage disposals, especially not for the family home. Kitchen scraps are valuable. If you absolutely have no other use for your kitchen scraps, then put them into your compost pit or worm farm. The compost pit and/or worm farm

Julie next to one of the many composters.

provides you with rich garden soil as well as the means to naturally dispose of your kitchen scraps. There are many, many possible designs, so do your research on what type will work best for you.

GRASS CLIPPINGS

Grass clippings are one of the best garden mulches you can get. They can be spread lightly around the bases of plants. The clippings help to keep in moisture and to promote the proliferation of earthworms. Spread thickly on top of unwanted wild grass and weeds, it will kill off most everything underneath, enabling you to plant other plants within a few months.

For the record, I don't see any value in maintaining a lawn, so we never have grass clippings of our own to use for composting or mulch. However, lawns are still a thing, so it's very easy to get bags of lawn clippings from others. Do not obtain grass clippings that have been treated with pesticides.

TREE ORNAMENTS

We have a tradition of making Christmas, Hanukkah, and Kwanzaa ornaments every year. Everyone really enjoys doing this.

The process is completely open to interpretation. Start with the materials that you have, and they can help provide design ideas.

Gather various materials such as twist ties, to make colorful chain-link garlands; last year's Christmas cards, to repurpose the images; metallic cardboard and foil that comes with certain food packaging, to fashion stars and other symbols; small plastic yogurt containers or other cups, which can become bells when decorated. Even old

A view of a tree decorated with ornaments made from common discards.

aluminum pie pans cut in a spiral can become a lovely dangling ornament.

An ornament is created from the lid of a can by carefully cutting it into a creative shape.

You'll also need scissors, tape and/or glue, colored markers, and paper clips or string for hanging the ornaments. Meaningful symbols make good design ideas: stars, wreaths, trees, wise men, Madonna and child, snowflakes, bells, and candles for Christmas; menorahs for Hanukkah; the Kinara and fruits for Kwanzaa.

This is just the tip of the iceberg of what you can recycle into practical items. The more you can reuse different kinds of materials that you'd normally have discarded, the more you'll be part of the solution, and the better you'll feel about taking responsibility for the products you use.

The more you find value in these resources that you have been routinely discarding, the wealthier you'll be both spiritually and financially.

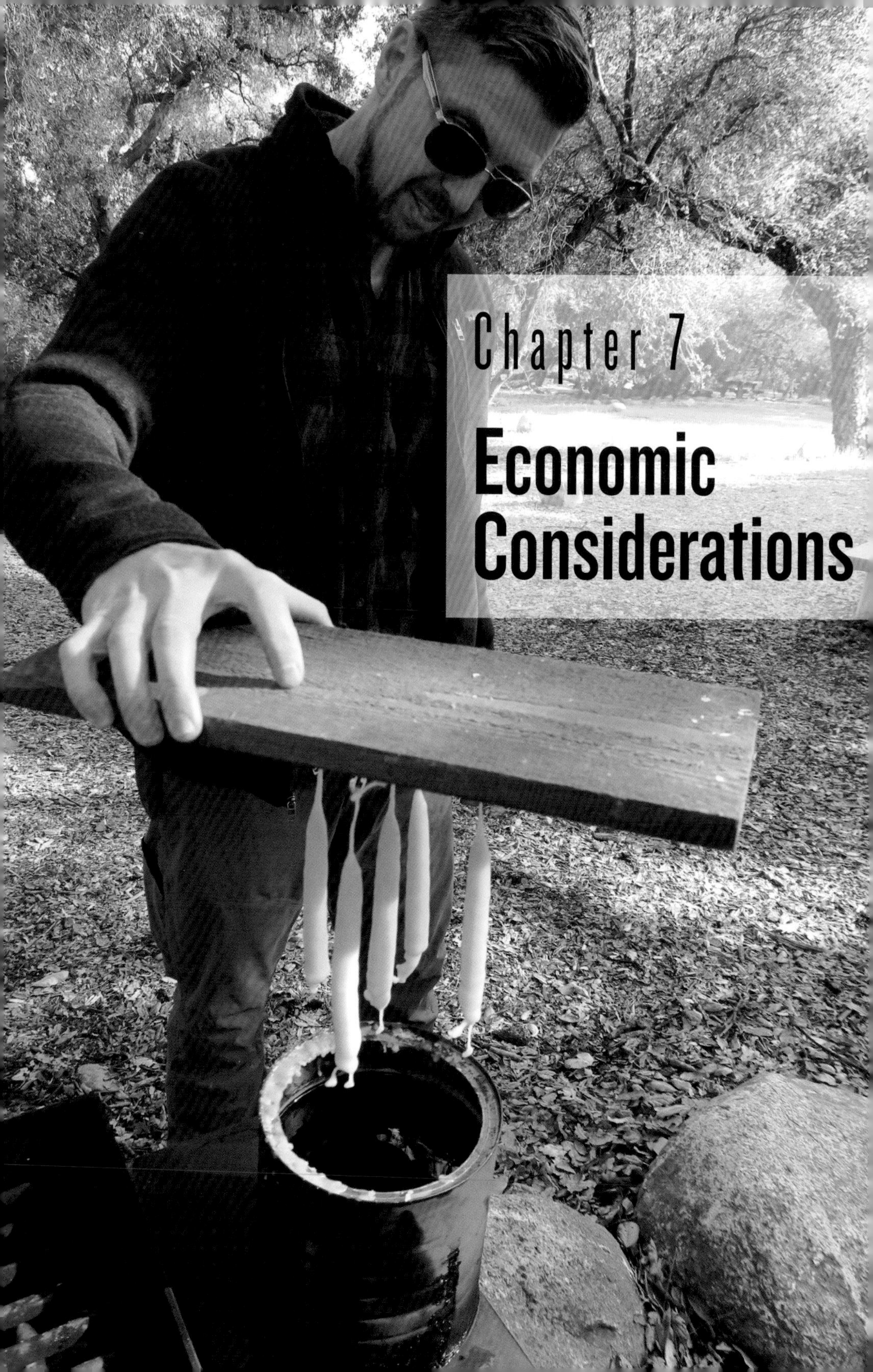

Chapter 7

Economic Considerations

For whatever reason, many survivalists rarely talk about the role of money in "survival." But there is a major industry of people who write books about every imaginable aspect of personal economics. You see them on TV shows and selling tickets to seminars, telling you that they have a secret to getting rich quick and retiring young.

The seminars are not cheap and do not actually contain anything that I'd call a secret—just lots of practical advice about the changing market. Whenever I've discussed the financial gurus and their countless get-rich-quick seminars with my husband, we've concluded that the only ones getting rich are the ones paid for holding the seminars.

What we're sharing here are some very, very basic guidelines for personal economic solvency.

> **IN A NUTSHELL**
>
> - Don't buy it if you don't really *need* it.
> - Get out of debt!
> - When money is tight, make a list of everything you can sell or barter.
> - Get to know your neighbors.
> - Join or start a Neighborhood Watch

MONEY

Too many of us rely on the ability to go to a bank or use an ATM regularly. Plus, most people use credit cards all the time, which is a technology that can only exist in an inter-connected world powered by electricity.

People have always figured out how to buy and sell and trade, even before there was electricity. But in a transition to no electricity, people might not have access to their money—maybe temporarily or maybe permanently, depending on the nature of the emergency.

Rural areas would do somewhat better, for a variety of reasons. People in rural areas have quite an advantage over people in urban centers since they are more likely to know where all their needs are coming from. They are also more likely to be producers of a raw commodity, with which they can directly trade for needs.

In urban areas, however, everyone tends to buy everything that's needed, and any food, animal, or craft production is nearly always hobby level at best.

A major disaster that takes out electricity will take out the ability for most urban residents to conduct ordinary transactions. During the interim, people should band together for protection, because you can expect violence, chaos, and unpredictability during such a period, until people figure out a new way of doing things.

Do not underestimate the severe impact that lack of access to money will have on your life and society. My suggestion is to constantly have in the back of your mind the questions, "What would I do if I could not get cash today? What can I do differently each day to be better prepared if that ever happened?"

There are many options, such as always having extra cash and coin on hand—well-hidden, of course. And always storing a little more of the basics than your family will need, so you have something extra for barter,

TOP BARTER ITEMS

- Toilet paper
- Alcohol (all forms, including the DIY variety)
- Chocolate (has a great shelf life)
- Coffee
- Tobacco (cigarettes, tobacco, loose)
- Aspirin (and various common medical supplies)
- First aid supplies (bandages, tape, disinfectant)
- Vitamins
- Food, canned goods
- Feminine supplies
- Soap (bar soap and liquid soap)
- Small sewing kits
- Batteries (ideally, rechargeables, since they can be recharged with a solar charger)

Julie's "home sweet home," where she lived frugally for 18 months.

if need be. In times of duress, the best barter items tend to be those that feed the vices: alcohol, tobacco, chocolate, coffee, sugar, salt, all of which have a great shelf life.

At a time when I wanted to save money, I lived in a simple tent to be able to pursue my personal training.

I learned along with other students from the creator of our non-profit, Richard White, that there are two ways to improve your economic power: earn more or spend less. Yes, everyone says they want to do both. Spending less is harder than most of us think, especially if we have children who are crying for the latest gadget, toy, or article of clothing that their friends have. Or one spouse of a married couple might be very disciplined, but the other can't live without some trinket or gadget. I know it's very difficult.

Incidentally, "Beanie Babies," a small beanbag stuffed-animal toy, were all the rage when my son was in elementary school. I shared with him an article on how the trend was foisted onto the children's market. *Zillions*, a money-focused children's magazine produced by Consumer Reports, explained how the Beanie Babies business investors' goal was very clear: get as much money as possible as quickly as possible by creating a demand for the item.

After reading the article, my son emerged better able to be alert to quality and to listen to his own feelings (as opposed to the marketing and intense peer pressure). I strongly recommend teaching children to better understand money, savvy consumerism, and marketing early. Unfortunately, *Zillions* stopped being produced in 2000.

At any age, it's always sound advice to do whatever you can to cut expenses, and to pay off debt! Whatever (within ethicality and morality, of course)!

Let's explore some ways in which you can generate some extra cash. Remember, these are just basic ideas. You must see what works for you, and then run with it.

THINGS YOU CAN MAKE AND SELL

If you can make something that people want, you will probably always have some income from it. Lots of people make soap, candles, woven bags, food items, clothing, and leather goods, etc. If you make something that people actually need, you will always have a market for your products.

Arts and crafts—wooden carvings, wreaths, cards, metal crafts, baskets—are a little more speculative, because you're creating something that no one *needs*. And part of your challenge will be to convince people that they don't just want your arts and crafts, they actually need them! Sometimes that works, sometimes it doesn't. However, if you really love to do these crafts, and you do them well, you might make a name for yourself, and people will buy them and pay you well because you made it!

There are a handful of potters, basket makers, and artists who command a great price for their work. Keep in mind that if you pursue this path, you

Patience's tatting art—a beautiful and highly sellable craft.

will spend a lot of time just promoting yourself and your work, with no real guarantee that it will all pay off. But if you really believe in yourself, go for it!

THINGS YOU CAN GROW OR PREPARE

Food is one of the major categories of products that everyone needs. If you just have a small farm or a backyard garden, you won't be competing with any of the big chain grocery stores or factory farms. But you can still create a niche product that could provide income for your family. The key is to get to know what's out there. Be observant to what people are selling and at what prices in trendy stores, in farmers markets, and online.

Do you have something that you can grow as a fresh vegetable, fruit, or herb? Can you pack and ship it? Do you know how to can vegetables and make jams? You can market your canned goods under a custom label and create at least a local following and demand for your product.

I didn't say you'd get rich doing this—just that you can avoid being poor. You could also consider buying products in bulk wholesale, and then repackaging them under your label. That's exactly what retailers do!

SERVICES YOU CAN OFFER

When you're in the position of needing more income, and you don't particularly want a full-time job working at someone else's business, you should make a list of all your abilities, skills, and talents.

Just write them all out on a paper, whatever they may be, both hobbies and trained skills.

Prudence's home business is Prudent Pastries.

Julie often teaches and lectures, a skill that can be applied and practiced just about anywhere.

Write them all out so you can look at them objectively: auto mechanic, cook, gardener, tree pruner, wine maker, electrician, nurse, teacher, editor, musician, woodworker, etc. Everyone's list will be different. Your job is to decide which of your skills you can market. Prioritize using those skills you'd really like to do more often.

A friend of mine knew a man who loved working on cars, and when he finally opened his own shop, he *hated* it and couldn't wait to sell off his business. You see, he derived great pleasure from his involvement with automobiles, their history, what makes them tick, and

This woman creates original greeting cards, which she sells at local fairs.

talking with friends about various cars and fixes for common problems. But once he had a shop, everyone had a complaint. Everyone wanted

These ladies make crocheted products, which they then sell at local open-air markets.

the work done more cheaply and more quickly, and the complaints were overwhelming. So you want to go choose a path that you will love and love getting up in the morning to pursue.

Once you make your list of abilities, skills, and talents, circle the top three that you want to pursue.

Then, you make another list of at least three ways you can move forward with each of your chosen three talents. That means you must see where someone will hire you or pay for your services. Then you need to advertise in every way you can, preferably starting with all the possible free advertising.

HOW TO SELL YOUR PRODUCTS IN YOUR NEIGHBORHOOD

Start your business enterprise in your own immediate neighborhood. You can talk to neighbors and give them a flier about what you sell and how they can acquire your services. Make it easy for people to say "yes."

In the neighborhood where our non-profit headquarters is located, our members have engaged our neighbors in numerous home businesses, beginning with selling eggs door-to-door when we had many chickens. We've also sold potted plants, booklets, honey, edible cactus, and fruits in this same manner. We've sold sewing and cleaning services this way.

Another effective local approach is having a booth at the end of your driveway or on the parkway. We have done this with our various sales items between specific times on a consistent day of the week when our sidewalk stand was regularly open. The idea that is most beneficial for everyone is to sell items that are not only attractive and professionally presented, but that also come with educational product descriptions and meaningful, creative touches. Selling the useable good idea along with the actual item enhances it in the eyes of others. They too will likely recognize the value there.

For instance, share how honey is a whole food, or why certain produce or healthy pastries are wholesome or support your health.

Yard sales and flea markets can be avenues for selling your items and services, as well as being very good publicity. It's worth a try.

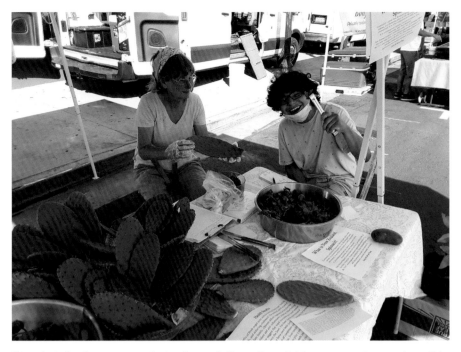

Stand at the farmers market, where Julie sells prickly pear cactus pads, wild foods, and other natural products, with volunteer Saul Sernas.

I've also had an honor system where people would buy a plant and just leave the cash money in an envelope in the mailbox and then call to let me know. Then, I would go to the mailbox and collect. This can be more effective than you might expect.

In addition, since a local Neighborhood Watch was organized, we got to know all our neighbors and began working with them.

I'm aware that some of you will recoil at going to your neighbors and trying to sell products or services: "What will my neighbors think of me? Won't they assume I am poor?"

I am well aware of these concerns, but whether this is a real concern or not depends on your neighborhood and the people who live there. One of my associates reported that when he lived in a small rural town, it was common to offer canned goods, produce, repair services, plumbing and electrical services, and auto repair at discounted prices to neighbors. Of course, the economics of a small town is very different than living in a city for some obvious reasons.

WTI Survival Shop flea market booth.

I have had primarily very positive feedback from my attempts to reach out and find a mutually beneficial solution to an economic hardship.

BARTER A SKILL

Regardless of what you do day in and out for income, you should always have a backup skill or ability to make something that would be in some demand if the normal functioning of society disappeared. Here are some examples of those types of skills: reupholstering furniture, fixing cars, fixing bicycles, plumbing, electrical work, courier service, protection services, repairing firearms, locksmithing, washing clothes, making clothes, blacksmithing/metalsmithing, etc. Here are some of the things you could make that would always be in demand: alcohol (beer and

Javier making candles.

Alfonso fixing a bike.

wine, or medical-grade alcohol, which requires distillation), soups, dried vegetables, canned goods, clothing, soaps, candles, etc.

Usually, there is no way to know in advance which skill, or which product, will be the most in-demand. But by studying the details of what happens during wartime, or times of severe economic depression, you will realize that if the things we ordinarily take for granted are suddenly not there, someone can earn their keep by filling that need.

SOCIAL INTERACTIONS

Some people think that they will be a Rambo and do everything themselves after a disaster. If you're capable of that, well, good luck to you! But in my opinion, you'll do far better by developing as many contacts and relationships as possible right now, since these contacts with other people can be a lifeline when things go sour. Plus, working with other people to solve problems is far more fulfilling and enjoyable than going it alone.

For instance, in many cultures washing clothes together has provided a time to commune with friends, family, and neighbors. Historically, the same went for making clothes and growing and processing foods together. This meant people were able to share their feelings, hopes, and concerns and were potentially able to better support one another.

We've all heard the expression that when one door closes, another opens. That all depends. In part, it depends on what made that door close in the first place.

But in the context of our discussion here, it's important to see the world as it really is. What does it mean when one door closes? It can mean that you got fired from a job, that a comet hit your part of town, or that someone close to you died. It can mean a lot of things. So, in terms of "doors opening," it's important to realize that nearly everything in your life happens as a result of your interactions with other people, and with their interactions with you. People who say, "I am not a people person" are those who tend to keep doors closed all around them. It is actually very important from a survival and self-reliance standpoint to have broad interactions with people of all economic classes and all races and all diverse backgrounds, as much as is possible and feasible.

Your willingness to be open to different people, and to find areas of commonality, will go a very long way to making doors open in your life when you need them opened. In other words, when one door closes, another may or may not open for you—but the more contacts with people that you've made, the broader your possibilities—your "doors" that you will then be able to "open."

That's one reason I've found working at the farmer's market and getting to know the people in my community have been wonderful opportunities for mutual growth and benefits.

Everything is about people, not things.

SIMPLE STEPS YOU CAN TAKE

In a survival situation, you must act wisely, often quickly, and without mistakes. You also will likely need to make hard decisions about what you should and should not do. I am a great fan of writing a list of all the things

I need to do daily and prioritizing it. This is even more important in a survival setting, where you might not be able to think clearly. Write a list and stick to your list as much as possible during the day.

Join your local Neighborhood Watch. Get to know your neighbors and become an active part of your local system of communication and preventing criminal activity. Your neighborhood doesn't have a NW? Start one! Need help getting started? Go to www.nnw.org.

Take your local CERT (Community Emergency Response Team) training. This is an excellent way to see who's who, and what systems will come into play, in the aftermath of an emergency in your community. You might be surprised to learn what sort of plans already exist for dealing with local emergencies. Find a local CERT training near you at www.ready.gov/cert.

Learn how to grow at least some of your own food. If you have absolutely no idea how to start, look for your local neighborhood garden or your local farmer. Check out gardening videos on YouTube. And get a gardening book at the library, such as any of the quality gardening books from Rodale Books.

Julie and Racina at shooting range.

Join a gun club, and learn how to safely and ethically use a firearm. How do you find a local gun club? Check online, or check explore.nra.org /programs/clubs/ for local clubs and ranges. If you haven't had firearm safety and competence training, get it, so you and others can be safe. Airguns are great for building skills because pellets are cheap. Always seek to deter rather than maim or kill.

All this being said, always avoid rather than exposing yourself to or participating in unnecessary violence.

Make the decision to learn a few new skills. Don't overthink this, and don't put it off! Just begin with those skills that interest you. This might mean taking some classes at a local community college or privately. I know you're already a very busy person with family and work and home, and I agree that education is expensive in many ways, but ignorance is even more expensive.

MONEY ALTERNATIVES

Sometimes, in certain unique circumstances, the members of a community have created their own alternative "money," a scrip that they circulate among themselves. We are aware of this occurring at a school, or in a remote community, and even in some developing countries where there are no banks.

This can be a viable solution for getting people to produce and exchange goods and get out of poverty. So that everyone buys into the program, it should be well thought-out to accommodate growth, and to take fraud into account. Such a system tends to work best when it stays small, like under five hundred people, but as it grows, your community should probably consider forming a credit union–style bank.

A COMMUNITY PERSPECTIVE

It's very insightful to note how many "survivalists" talk about escaping to rural areas and to wilderness areas. Though I have nothing against such action, that is not currently my path. Historically, cities developed when people came together to trade, to exchange ideas, to promote the common good. Cities are not necessarily a bad thing, and through the course of humankind, they have played a role for the good and betterment of those who supported the city.

The structures that have been built up in the cities, over centuries, are mechanisms of survival. They are institutions and methodologies that promote education, health, security, and economic growth. But this is not always the case, and bigger is not always better, especially when it comes to cities.

Still, I have found that my work is where other people are. I have chosen a path of spiritual, ethical, economical, and ecological living in the urban/suburban landscape.

If you choose to live in the urban setting, I strongly suggest that you become an active player in making your world a better place. Get involved in your Neighborhood Watch, which was developed so that neighbors can get to know each other, work together, and communicate, and reduce criminal activities in their midst. If Neighborhood Watch does not exist in your neighborhood, go start one!

As the urban activist David Hereford said, "The level of crime in a neighborhood is inversely proportionate to the level of communication among the neighbors."

Although there are many problems to be concerned with in the world, doing as much as we can will enable each of us to take more steps forward. Your community and I sincerely support your efforts!

Reading List and Resources

ABCs of Beekeeping, Roda Shope. Beautiful children's book with exquisite photography and illustrations.

Beekeeping for Beginners: How to Raise Your First Bee Colonies, Amber Bradshaw.

Diet for a Small Planet (50th Anniversary Edition), Frances Moore Lappé. Excellent practical guide for combining grains and legumes for complete protein intake, with recipes from many cultures.

Extreme Simplicity: Homesteading in the City, Christopher Nyerges. Shows how Nyerges and his wife produced food and power, and dealt with preparedness in an urban setting.

Famine and Survival in America, Howard J. Ruff. A classic on the reasons for food storage.

The Honey Bee Hobbyist: The Care and Keeping of Bees, Norman Gary. Entertaining and extensive introduction to beekeeping. See also website HoneybeeHobbyist.com

How to Survive Anywhere, Christopher Nyerges. Covers how to address all basic needs, and more, with a wilderness focus.

Lights Out: A Cyberattack, A Nation Unprepared, Surviving the Aftermath, Ted Koppel.

Mending Life: A Handbook for Repairing Clothes and Hearts, Nina and Sonya Montenegro. A beautiful modern sewing and mending guide with vibrant, full-color illustrations.

Natural Food Storage Bible: Secrets of Storing, Cooking and Enjoying Natural Foods, Sybil D. Hendricks and Sharon Dienstbier. Food storage without preservatives.

Passport to Survival, Esther Dickey. Explores the "survival four": wheat, powdered milk, salt, and honey, with recipes and total emergency preparedness.

Self-Sufficient Home, Christopher Nyerges. Shows how ordinary people produced their own power, grew their own food, collected rain, etc.

Stocking Up, Carol Hupping Stoner.

Urban Survival Guide, Christopher Nyerges.

Wheat for Man, Vernice Rosenvall. Excellent, easy-to-follow recipes.

For more information about Julie's books and classes please go to in-joysurvival.com

About the Author

Julie L. Jesseph-Balaa has studied and applied various aspects of permaculture and frugal living for decades. She is an executive board member of White Tower, Inc., an educational non-profit founded to research and disseminate information on all aspects of survival. Jesseph-Balaa lectures regularly on organic gardening, backyard emergency planning, frugal living, and other topics. She lives in Los Angeles, where she built her own greenhouse and grows plants that she sells at the local farmers market.

Index

Notes